MEN OF
WAR

GREAT MILITARY FIGURES
OF THE 20TH CENTURY

MEN OF
WAR

GREAT MILITARY FIGURES OF THE 20TH CENTURY

HARRISON HUNT

MALLARD PRESS

An imprint of BDD Promotional Book Company, Inc.,
666 Fifth Avenue, New York, New York, 10103

MALLARD
PRESS

An imprint of BDD Promotional Book
Company, 666 Fifth Avenue, New York,
New York 10103

Copyright © 1991 by M & M Books

ISBN 0-7924-5418-9

AN M&M BOOK

Men of War was prepared and produced
by M & M Books, 11 W. 19th Street,
New York, New York 10011

Project Director & Editor: Gary Fishgall

Senior Editorial Assistant: Shirley
Vierheller; Editorial Assistants: Maxine
Dormer, Ben D'Amprisi, Jr.; Copyediting:
Bert N. Zelman, Keith Walsh of Publish-
ers Workshop Inc; Photo Research:
Maxine Dormer.

Designer: Binns & Lubin

Separations and Printing: Regent
Publishing Services Ltd.

(Preceeding pages) Gen. Douglas
MacArthur (seated in front seat) and his
aide, Col. Lloyd Lehrbas, inspect the
ruins of a town on Leyte Island in
October, 1944.

(These pages) The U.S. army rolls into
Germany during World War II. GIs under
Gen. Omar Bradley first penetrated the
Reich in September 1944.

CONTENTS

INTRODUCTION

SINCE TIME IMMEMORIAL, war has paradoxically brought out the worst and the best in people, inspiring unspeakable acts of cruelty and almost superhuman deeds of heroism. In no age has the dual nature of combat been more evident than during the 20th century, which has seen warfare—declared or undeclared—somewhere on the globe virtually throughout its span of years, including the two most devastating wars in history. *Men of War* tells the stories of the key figures in these conflicts, men who have made indelible contributions to the art of war.

Spanning the period from the Boer War to the present, *Men of War* chronicles an era of rapid changes in military science, changes unparalleled by those of any other age. The first engagements of the century featured cavalry charges. The automobile—much less the tank—had not come into widespread use, and the airplane had not yet been invented. In the intervening years warfare has become ever more mechanized, with the introduction of high-speed fighter planes, elite strike forces, electronic tracking, and, of course, that ultimate product of military technology, the nuclear bomb. While it is not within the scope of this book to chronicle the changing nature of warfare, some aspects of technological progress can be glimpsed in the fascinating stories of such seminal figures as George Patton, Hap Arnold, Roger Keyes, and Isoroku Yamamoto. More importantly perhaps, the 90 individuals portrayed in *Men of War* convincingly illustrate that, *despite* changing technology, individual achievement, like that of Audie Murphy and Vo Nguyen Giap, remains a key factor in determining victory or defeat. Indeed the role of the individual remains as crucial to warfare in the 20th century as it did in the days of Alexander, Caesar, and Napoleon.

In order to better illustrate some of the essential qualities that characterize individuals in combat, *Men of War*

is uniquely organized into four thematic sections. This approach, rather than one based on chronology, will enable the reader to compare and contrast military men with similar missions throughout the century. We begin with High Command, which examines the careers of the world's top strategists, from Horatio Kitchener to Dwight D. Eisenhower to Maxwell Taylor. Fighting Men spotlights 19 soldiers and sailors whose exploits have become legendary. Among them are Alvin York, Lawrence of Arabia, Eddie Rickenbacker, and John F. Kennedy. Rebels examines the lives of such famed guerrillas and revolutionaries as Pancho Villa, Leon Trotsky, and Mao Zedong. Finally Leaders of Men looks at the field commanders, like Jacques LeClerc, Erwin Rommel, Mustafa Kemal, and Moshe Dayan, who inspired their followers through the force of their personalities as well as their military genius. Given our truly international cast—which includes representatives from Europe, North America, South America, Asia, Australia, and Africa—the reader can quickly identify the figures profiled in these four sections by examining the headings, which include the subject's highest military rank, lifespan, and country of service. The nationalities are further highlighted by the use of flags which, for ease of identification, are the standards currently in use. The notable exception is the use of the flag of the Third Reich. Clearly in this case the colors of either East or West Germany would have been inappropriate.

Selecting the 90 individuals chronicled in *Men of War* from hundreds of viable candidates was a complex task. The editor and I have chosen a representative sampling from conflicts throughout the century, although commanders and fighting men from the First and Second World Wars naturally predominate. While we have selected figures from each major branch of service, the nature of modern warfare mandates that the world's armies get the lion's share of space. The individuals in each section were chosen solely on the basis of their military accomplishments, without regard to their successes or failures in other endeavors. They run the gamut from the internationally acclaimed—

Douglas MacArthur and Bernard Montgomery, among them—to little-known heroes like "Fighting Fred" Funston and Sir Claude MacDonald. The stories of the latter may even be new to dedicated military history buffs. Some of the choices were extremely difficult. Of the "Big Four" leaders of the Second World War—Franklin D. Roosevelt, Winston Churchill, Joseph Stalin, and Chiang Kai-shek—only FDR is not included in this book. The reason is that, while Roosevelt was undeniably a pivotal wartime figure, he played a much less active role in detailed strategic planning than did the others, leaving most of the major military decisions to his Army Chief of Staff, George C. Marshall. Thus Marshall *is* included. Conversely, Lord Alanbrooke, Marshall's British counterpart, has been excluded in favor of his boss, Sir Winston Churchill.

No less difficult than determining the 90 people chronicled herein was the selection of photographs to illustrate their careers. By the turn of the century, the art of photography had become well established and many of the figures profiled in this volume were well documented on film. The images chosen for this volume—formal portraits and action scenes—combine to capture each man's character as well as to illustrate some of the century's most significant conflicts.

In a survey of this scope the biographies are, of necessity, brief. Each profile can be looked upon as an introduction to the life and military career of one of these fascinating individuals. If you—like the author—find yourself captivated by some of them, numerous book-length biographies and campaign studies are readily available.

Omar Bradley—known as the "GI's general"—during World War II.

CHRONOLOGY OF 20TH-CENTURY MILITARY EVENTS

1900

February 15 Boer siege of Kimberley, South Africa, broken

February 28 British forces secure Ladysmith, South Africa

March 23 Philippine Insurrection leader Emilio Aguinaldo captured by U.S. forces

May 31 British capture Johannesburg, South Africa

June 5 Fall of Pretoria, South Africa

June 30 Chinese Boxers begin 55-day siege of foreign legations in Peking

August 14 Allied relief forces enter Peking

1902

May 31 Treaty of Vereeniging ends Boer War

1904

February 8 Japanese attack Russian fleet at Port Arthur, China, beginning Russo-Japanese War

August 7–January 2, 1905 Japanese siege of Port Arthur

August 10 Battle of the Yellow Sea

1905

May 27 Battle of Tsushima

1906

September 6 Treaty of Portsmouth ends Russo-Japanese War

1911

September 29 Italy declares war on Turkey

October 11 Italian forces invade Libya

1912

October 15 Treaty of Ouchy ends Italo-Turkish War

1914

April 21 United States forces raid Vera Cruz, Mexico

June 28 Austro-Hungarian Archduke Francis Ferdinand assassinated in Sarajevo, Bosnia, precipitating the First World War

August 2–4 Belgium and Luxembourg invaded by Germany

August 20–25 Battle of the Ardennes

August 26–30 Battle of Tannenberg

September 5–10 First Battle of the Marne

October 18–November 22 First Battle of Ypres

October 26 Forces under Pancho Villa and Emiliano Zapata capture Mexico City

October 29 Turkey enters First World War

December 8 Battle of the Falkland Islands

1915

April 22–May 25 Second Battle of Ypres

April 25–January 9, 1916 Gallipoli campaign, Turkey

May 7 *Lusitania* sunk off Ireland by German U-boat

1916

February 21–December 18 Battle of Verdun

March 9 Pancho Villa raids Columbus, New Mexico

March 15–February 5, 1917 U.S. Gen. John J. Pershing leads punitive expedition against Pancho Villa in Mexico

April 24 Easter Uprising, Dublin, Ireland

May 31–June 1 Battle of Jutland

June 5 Arabs capture Medina

June 24–November 13 First Battle of the Somme

1917

March 12 Russian Revolution begins

April 6 The United States enters First World War

November 7 Bolshevik Revolution begins in Russia

December 9 British forces capture Jerusalem from Turks

1918

March 3 Treaty of Brest-Litovsk ends war between Germany and Soviet Russia

April 23 British raid on Zeebrugge, the Netherlands

May 30–June 17 Battles of Château-Thierry and Belleau Wood

July 15–17 Second Battle of the Marne

August 8–September 4 Amiens offensive

September 26–November 11 Meuse-Argonne offensive

October 1 Allied forces capture Damascus from Turks

October 30 Turkey signs Armistice

November 11 Germany signs Armistice

1919

June 28 Treaty of Versailles ends First World War

November 26 Irish revolution begins

1928

August 27 Kellogg-Briand Pact outlaws war

1932

January 28 Japan begins invasion of Manchuria

1935

October 3–February 17, 1916 Italian forces conquer Ethiopia

1936

March 7 German troops occupy Rhineland demilitarized zone

July 18 Spanish Civil War begins

1937

April 25 Bombing of Guernica, Spain by German Kondor Legion

July 7 Sino-Japanese War begins

July 28 Japanese capture Peking

November 11 Japanese capture Shanghai

1938

March 12 German troops occupy Austria

October 21 Japanese capture Canton

1939

January 26 Franco's forces capture Barcelona

March 10–16 Germany invades Czechoslovakia

March 28 Madrid and Valencia surrender to Franco

September 1 Germany invades Poland, beginning Second World War

September 17 Soviet troops invade eastern Poland

1940

May 10 German invasion of Low Countries and France begins

May 28–June 4 Evacuation of Allied troops from Dunkirk, France

June 10 Italy enters the war

June 21 France surrenders to Germany

August 8–October 30 Battle of Britain

1941

May 28 German battleship *Bismarck* sunk

June 22 Germany invades Soviet Union

September 26 Germans capture Kiev

December 7 Japanese attack Pearl Harbor

December 22 Japan launches invasion of Luzon, Philippines

December 25 Japanese capture Hong Kong

1942

February 15 Japanese capture Singapore

April 18 U.S. planes bomb Tokyo

May 6 Corregidor falls to the Japanese

May 7–8 Battle of the Coral Sea

June 4–6 Battle of Midway

June 21 Germans capture Tobruk, Libya

August 7–February 7, 1943 Battle of Guadalcanal

August 24–February 2, 1943 Battle of Stalingrad

October 23–November 4 Battle of El Alamein, Egypt

1943

March 6 Battle of Medenine, Tunisia

July 9–10 Allied invasion of Sicily

September 9 Allied forces land at Salerno, Italy

1944

January 19 German siege of Leningrad broken

January 22 Allied forces land at Anzio, Italy

June 4 Allies capture Rome

June 6 Allied invasion of Normandy

August 15 Allied invasion of southern France

August 25 Allies liberate Paris

October 19 American forces begin liberation of the Philippines

December 16–January 16, 1945 Battle of the Bulge

1945

May 2 Red Army captures Berlin

May 8 Germany surrenders

August 6 & 9 Atomic bombs dropped on Hiroshima and Nagasaki

September 2 Japan surrenders, ending Second World War

1948

May 15–January 7, 1949 Israeli War for Independence

September 14–24 Battle of Tsinan, China

October 27–November 1 Battle of Mukden, China

1949

January 22 Peking falls to Chinese Communists

October 15 Canton captured by Chinese Communists

December 7 Chinese Nationalists withdraw to Taiwan

1950

June 25 North Korean forces invade the South

September 15–25 United Nations forces land at Inchon, Korea

November 25–December 15 United Nations forces driven south of 38th parallel

1951

May 22–July 8 United Nations counteroffensive

1952

March 10 Gen. Fulgencio Batista leads coup in Cuba

October 20–June 15, 1953 Mau Mau uprising, Kenya

1953

July 27 Korean armistice signed

November 20–May 7, 1954 Siege of Dienbienphu, Vietnam

1956

October 29–November 6 Suez War

1959

January 1 Fidel Castro siezes power in Cuba

1961

April 22-26 French army mutiny in Algeria

1964

August 2 North Vietnamese attack U.S. destroyer in the Gulf of Tonkin

1965

February 7 First attack against U.S. forces in South Vietnam, at Pleiku

1966

March 9 France withdraws from NATO

1967

June 5–10 Arab-Israeli Six-Day War

1968

January 21–April 8 Siege of Khe Sanh, Vietnam

January 30–February 29 Tet offensive

1969

September 1 Muammar Qaddafi stages coup in Libya

1970

November 21 U.S. forces raid Son Tay Prisoner-of-War camp

1971

January 25 Idi Amin seizes power in Uganda

December 3–16 India-Pakistan War

1973

March 29 Last U.S. troops leave Vietnam

October 6–24 Yom Kippur War between Israel and Egypt & Syria

1975

April 1 Danang falls to North Vietnamese forces

April 30 South Vietnam surrenders to the North

1979

April 11 Idi Amin overthrown in Uganda

December 24 Soviet forces begin their occupation of Afghanistan

1980

September 9 Iran-Iraq War begins

1982

April 2 Argentina invades Falkland Islands

June 14 Argentine forces surrender to British forces in the Falklands

1983

October 25 U.S. invasion of Grenada

1986

April 15 U.S. reprisal air raid on Libya

1989

February 15 Soviet troops withdraw from Afghanistan

December 20 U.S. invasion of Panama

1990

August 2 Iraq invades Kuwait

The Allied planning team for the Normandy invasion. From left, they are Gen. Omar Bradley; Adm. Sir Bertram Ramsay; Sir Arthur Tedder; Gen. Dwight D. Eisenhower; Sir Bernard Montgomery; Air Chief Marshal Sir Trafford Leigh-Mallory; and Gen. Walter Bedell Smith.

HIGH COMMAND

JOHN J. PERSHING

United States, 1860–1948

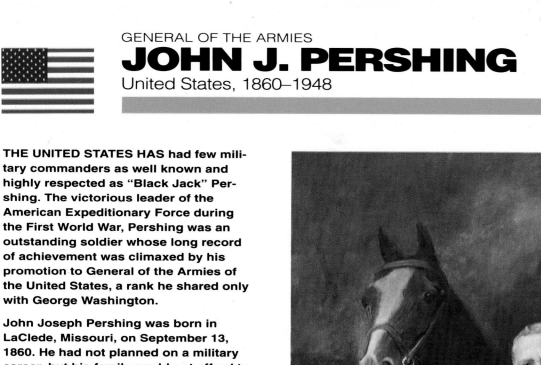

THE UNITED STATES HAS had military commanders as well known and highly respected as "Black Jack" Pershing. The victorious leader of the American Expeditionary Force during the First World War, Pershing was an outstanding soldier whose long record of achievement was climaxed by his promotion to General of the Armies of the United States, a rank he shared only with George Washington.

John Joseph Pershing was born in LaClede, Missouri, on September 13, 1860. He had not planned on a military career, but his family could not afford to send him to college, so he applied to the tuition-free U.S. Military Academy. Admitted to West Point in 1882, Pershing became a model cadet and was named First Captain in his senior year. Commissioned a cavalry lieutenant upon his graduation in 1886, he was assigned to bases in New Mexico and Nebraska, where he got his first combat experience fighting Indians. He later served as an officer with the African-American Tenth Cavalry in Montana, from which he earned the nickname "Black Jack."

During the Spanish-American War, Pershing—still a lieutenant—served in Cuba, distinguishing himself at the Battles of San Juan Hill and Santiago. At the conclusion of the fighting there in 1899 he volunteered for duty in the Philippines, where he joined the force that put down the last remnants of the Filipino insurrection in Mindanao, finally earning promotion to captain in 1901 as a result. Pershing's long wait for advancement was more than compensated for in 1905, however, when he was assigned as American observer to the Russo-Japanese War. His reports and service record so impressed President Theodore Roosevelt that he jumped the captain directly to brigadier general.

When Pancho Villa started raiding villages in New Mexico in 1916, Gen. Frederick Funston sent Pershing across the border to stop the Mexican revolutionary. Although Pershing's campaign against Villa was a failure due to the excessive limitations imposed upon "Black Jack" by the State Department, it proved that he was a first-rate field commander and led to his appointment as head of the American Expeditionary Force (AEF) when the United States

Pershing and his staff en route to France aboard the White Star liner *Baltic* in June 1917.

(Opposite) "Black Jack" Pershing, beloved commander of the American Expeditionary Force during World War I, in an oil painting from 1920/21 by Douglas Volk.

entered the World War in 1917. Pershing directed the mobilization and training of the 4.5 million American soldiers who served during the war years and led them throughout their campaigns in Europe. His careful planning proved itself in his doughboys' first major action at the Second Battle of the Marne on July 18, 1918, when they successfully spearheaded the Allied counteroffensive against the German line. Following this victory, Pershing's troops captured the strategic St-Mihiel salient in mid-September and played the decisive role in the Argonne offensive which brought an end to the war on November 11, 1918. The victorious American commander was subsequently rewarded

with promotion to General of the Armies on September 3, 1919.

After the AEF was demobilized Pershing returned to Washington, D.C., where he served as Army Chief of Staff until his retirement from active duty on his 64th birthday, in 1924. In 1931 "Black Jack" published his memoirs of the Great War, winning the Pulitzer Prize in History. General Pershing died in Washington at the age of 87 on July 15, 1948, and is buried in Arlington National Cemetery.

Gen. Pershing leading the American campaign against Pancho Villa in Mexico, 1916. The reputation he gained as a first-rate field commander during this operation earned him his appointment as head of the American forces in the Great War.

KARL DOENITZ
Germany, 1891–1980

IN MARKED CONTRAST to its emphasis on the battle fleet in the First World War, Germany placed little reliance on its surface navy during the 1939–1945 conflict. Rather, it relied primarily upon the submarine force of Adm. Karl Doenitz to carry on the fight against Allied shipping. For his part, Doenitz developed the Nazi's U-boat arm into one of Germany's most impressive fighting forces, nearly winning the Battle of the Atlantic for the Third Reich in the early years of the war.

Karl Doenitz was born on September 16, 1891, in Grünau-bei-Berlin, Germany. He entered the Imperial Navy as a sea cadet in 1910, earning an officer's commission three years later. Doenitz received his submarine training during the First World War, commanding a U-boat in the Mediterranean until his capture in 1918. He remained in the navy after Germany's capitulation, serving as a torpedo boat officer. He also surreptitiously instructed submarine crews, pretending to merely offer antisubmarine training since submersibles were banned to Germany under the Treaty of Versailles. When Adolf Hitler decided to openly defy the treaty in 1935 by rearming Germany, Doenitz was assigned to organize the Nazi U-boat service. Convincing Hitler of the strategic importance of submarine warfare, he succeeded in building a fleet of 57 U-boats by the beginning of the Second World War, increasing their number to more than 300 by 1942.

Doenitz organized his command into squads which preyed on Allied shipping as far away as the coast of the United States. These "wolf packs" proved immensely successful, sinking some 7 million tons of shipping. Recognizing Doenitz's tremendous contribution to the Nazi war effort, Hitler promoted him to admiral in 1942 and to grand admiral commanding the entire German navy on January 30, 1943. Despite his best efforts, however, the incredible production of American and British shipyards during the war years, coupled with the invention of sonar, slowly tipped the scales of naval superiority in favor of the Allies, and by the end of 1943 Doenitz realized that

(Right) Adm. Karl Doenitz, the mastermind behind Nazi Germany's highly successful U-boat compaign against Allied shipping.

(Above) Doenitz, seen here reviewing the troops, succeeded Adolf Hitler as head of the Third Reich in April 1945.

Germany could no longer win control of the Atlantic.

Admiral Doenitz continued to serve as one of Hitler's most trusted lieutenants until the end of the war, and on the Fuehrer's suicide in April 1945 succeeded him as head of state. On May 23, 15 days after Germany officially surrendered to the Allies, he was taken into custody by the British army. Convicted of war crimes at the Nuremberg Trials in 1946, he served ten years in Spandau Prison. Karl Doenitz died in Hamburg, West Germany, on December 24, 1980, one of the last surviving mem-

LORD LOUIS MOUNTBATTEN

United Kingdom, 1900–1979

THE LIFE OF Adm. Louis Mountbatten can be summed up in three words: dedication to duty. A high-ranking member of England's royal family, he could have lived a life of leisure, but his unflagging sense of duty led him instead to a distinguished career in the Royal Navy.

Lord Louis Mountbatten was born Prince Louis Francis Albert Victor Nicholas of Battenberg in Windsor, England, on June 25, 1900. His mother, Princess Victoria, was a granddaughter of Queen Victoria, and his father, an admiral in the Royal Navy, was Prince Louis of Battenberg. During the First World War anti-German sentiment in England led the elder Battenberg to renounce his German titles (as well as his position as British First Sea Lord) and anglicize the family name to Mountbatten.

Following in his father's footsteps, Louis Mountbatten entered the Royal Navy at the age of 13. After attending the Naval Colleges at Osborne and Dartmouth the 16-year-old midshipman served on both cruisers and submarines during the First World War, gaining valuable experience but seeing no combat. In the postwar years Mountbatten complemented his maritime experience with studies in electronics at Cambridge University, making him one of the Royal Navy's leading communications experts. Subsequently he served on destroyers, in the Admiralty's air division, and as personal aide to his cousins King Edward VII and King George VI.

At the outset of the Second World War, Lord Mountbatten, by then a captain, proved himself a determined, almost recklessly brave destroyer commander in combat in the North Sea and the Mediterranean. His personal courage and broad-based knowledge subsequently made him a natural choice for director of the United Kingdom's commandos following the retirement of Admiral Sir Roger Keyes in October 1941. As head of British Combined (interservice) Operations holding the temporary ranks of vice admiral, lieutenant general, and air marshal, Lord Mountbatten organized several raids on Norway and France in 1941 and 1942. The lessons learned in these early

assaults on the Nazis' "Fortress Europe" proved invaluable in planning the D-Day invasion two years later.

Mountbatten was not to take part in the final attack on Hitler's Reich, however. In August 1943 he was elevated to Supreme Allied Commander in Southeast Asia, where for the remainder of the war he successfully coordinated campaigns against the Japanese in India, Malaya, Indonesia, southern China, and particularly Burma, where desperate battles were fought. In recognition of his accomplishments in the

After the Japanese surrender Mountbatten was named the last English Viceroy of India, skillfully steering the British colony to its independence in August 1947. On his return to England he was appointed commander of NATO forces in the Mediterranean, and in 1955 he became England's First Sea Lord with the rank of admiral of the fleet. He finished his military career in 1965 as chief of the British Defense Staff. Lord Mountbatten was assassinated on August 27, 1979, when his yacht was blown up off the coast of Mullaghmore, Ireland, by Irish Republican Army

(Opposite) Lord Louis Mount-batten, the efficient Supreme Allied Commander in Southeast Asia, shortly after his appointment to the post in 1943.

(Right) Lord Mountbatten (center) in Karachi with the Governor General of Pakistan. After World War II, Lord Mountbatten served as the last British Viceroy of the Raj, overseeing independence for both India and Pakistan.

PAUL VON HINDENBURG

Germany, 1847–1934

PAUL VON HINDENBURG is a classic example of how the members of an army's high command can inspire confidence. Although his role as a tactician and strategist during the First World War was not substantial, the veteran soldier was invaluable to the German war effort as a symbol of victory and national determination.

Paul Ludwig Hans Anton von Beneckendorff und von Hindenburg was born into an aristocratic, or Junker, family in Posen, Prussia (now Poznán, Poland), on October 2, 1847. As a boy he attended military school at Wahlstatt, and upon his graduation in 1866 was commissioned a lieutenant in the Third Infantry. He served as a line officer during the Austro-Prussian War in 1866 and the Franco-Prussian War in 1870, winning decorations for bravery, including the Iron Cross, in both actions. Although he was not considered a particularly brilliant officer von Hindenburg rose steadily through the ranks, and at the time of his retirement in 1911 he was serving as a brigadier general in command of the German Fourth Army Corps.

When the First World War broke out in 1914 von Hindenburg was recalled to duty and assigned command of the Eighth Army in East Prussia, on the Russian front. On August 26–29 and September 9–10, his forces quickly decimated the Russian army at the Battles of Tannenberg and Masurian Lakes. Although the tactical planning for these campaigns—the first major German victories of the war—were handled almost entirely by his chief of staff, Gen. Erich Ludendorff, and other subordinates, the German public lay the credit for the victories at von Hindenburg's feet. Overnight, he became a national hero, and by November he was promoted to field marshal commanding the entire eastern front.

Field Marshal Paul von Hindenburg, the figurehead commander of the Kaiser's armies during World War I, in an oil portrait by Hans Best.

(Opposite) Hindenburg (left) reviewing war plans with Kaiser Wilhelm II (center) and Gen. Paul Ludendorff. Although Hindenburg bore the chief responsibility for the conduct of the war, he left most tactical decisions to Ludendorff, his chief of staff.

In 1916, when fighting on the western front came to a virtual standstill during the Battle of Verdun, von Hindenburg was appointed chief of the Imperial German staff and charged with the direction of the nation's overall war effort. As in the East, he permitted Ludendorff to make most of the tactical decisions, but as far as the German people were concerned the field marshal was in charge, and as such he inspired them to continue fighting for two more years. Von Hindenburg remained popular for the rest of the war, and even when defeat seemed inevitable he was hailed for calling for an armistice and restoring peace to his Fatherland.

Field Marshal von Hindenburg's popularity did not diminish after the war. The old Junker was elected president of the postwar German Weimar Republic in 1925, serving during the rise of the Nazi Party. In 1933, the feeble and easily influenced president was persuaded to name Adolf Hitler chancellor of Germany, thereby setting the stage for the onset of the Third Reich. On August 2, 1934, von Hindenburg died while in office at Neudeck, Germany; he was 86.

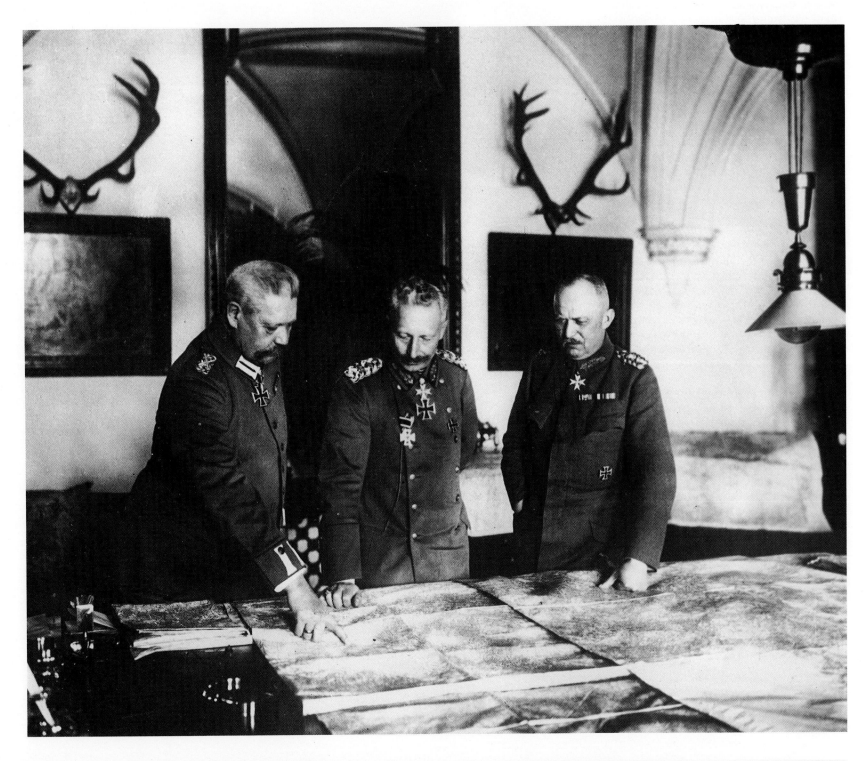

CHESTER NIMITZ

United States, 1885–1966

THE U.S. NAVY played its most decisive role of the century in the vast Pacific theater of the Second World War. The credit for the American victory there belongs in large part to the man who assumed command of the Pacific Fleet after Pearl Harbor, one of the war's great military leaders, Adm. Chester Nimitz.

Chester William Nimitz was born in Fredericksburg, Texas, on February 24, 1885. Inspired by his grandfather, a retired sea captain, he entered the U.S. Naval Academy at the age of 16. Commissioned an ensign in 1907, he spent the next 30 years serving on every type of vessel from submarines to battleships, rising to the rank of rear admiral in 1938.

When the United States began building up its armed forces in response to the outbreak of war in Europe in 1939, Admiral Nimitz was given responsibility for navy recruitment and training. His methodical approach greatly impressed Secretary of the Navy Frank Knox, and after the Japanese surprise attack at Pearl Harbor, Hawaii, decimated the Pacific Fleet on December 7, 1941, he was promoted to full admiral and commander in chief assigned to rebuild both the fleet and its morale. Proceeding with the painstaking attention to detail that characterized his career, he rapidly reestablished the navy's presence in the central Pacific, halting the Japanese advance toward Australia at the Battle of the Coral Sea on May 4–8, 1942. The following month, after the Japanese naval code had been broken, he placed three American carriers in ambush, and they dealt Adm. Isoroku Yamamoto's armada a crushing blow at the Battle of Midway, sinking four carriers from the Pearl Harbor attack. Going on the offensive the following year, Nimitz's forces turned the tide in the central Pacific in 1944, capturing the vital Japanese bases of Truk and Saipan and retaking the Philippines in conjunction with Gen. Douglas MacArthur's troops. In recognition of

(Above) Fleet Adm. Chester Nimitz, the insightful strategist behind the U.S. Naval victory in the Pacific in World War II.

(Right) Nimitz (center) paying a rare visit to the front on Guam in August 1944. The operational complexities of the vast Pacific theater usually forced him to remain at his headquarters in Pearl Harbor, Hawaii.

his outstanding contribution to these campaigns Nimitz was promoted to the five-star rank of fleet admiral.

By mid-1945 Nimitz's amphibious task forces had secured Iwo Jima and Okinawa, gaining clear control of the Pacific waters just south of Japan. After the Japanese surrender in September Nimitz was appointed U.S. Chief of Naval Operations. He retired from the service in 1947, after which he served on several United Nations committees and as a regent with the University of California. He died in San Francisco on February 20, 1966.

SIR WINSTON CHURCHILL

IN EVERY RESPECT, Sir Winston Churchill stands as the single most significant figure of the Allied war effort during the Second World War. His stirring wartime speeches gave immeasurable hope and support not only to Britain but to the entire free world, and his insight and diplomatic skill helped establish and hold together the alliance that won the war. In addition, as minister of defense, he played a key role in formulating British and Allied strategy, establishing himself as a master of high command.

Winston Leonard Spencer Churchill was born at Blenheim Palace, Woodstock, England, on November 30, 1874, the son of leading British politician Lord Randolph Churchill. Educated at Harrow, Winston had extreme difficulty with Latin so he was relegated to studying English, developing the command of the language that would later make him a world-famous author and orator. Subsequently entering the Royal Military Academy at Sandhurst, Churchill was commissioned a lieutenant in the Fourth Hussars in 1894. Thereafter he served in India and the Sudan, commanding a troop at the Battle of Omdurman in 1898.

(Opposite) Sir Winston Churchill, Britain's irrepressible wartime Prime Minister, in the uniform of an honorary Royal Air Force Commodore, an outfit that he often wore during the war years.

(Below) Churchill, seen here in his uniform as colonel-in-chief of the 4th Hussars, touring a portion of the German Siegfried Line in March 1945 with (from left) Field Marshal Montgomery, British Army Chief of Staff Sir Alan Brooke, an unidentified American, and Gen. William Simpson, commander of the U.S. 9th Army. Churchill visited more wartime fronts than any other Allied head of state.

The Prime Minister chats with Chief of Staff Sir Alan Brooke aboard a warship approaching the Normandy beachhead on June 11, 1944, just six days after the Allied invasion of France.

Promising "blood, toil, tears and sweat," Churchill vowed to lead Britain to victory, assuming also the duties of minister of defense. Within weeks of taking office he showed his determination to hang on, despite the fall of France, by ordering the remarkable flotilla that saved more than 300,000 troops from capture at Dunkirk in June and then overseeing the RAF's heroic defense in the Battle of Britain. Through the rest of the war Churchill played a major role in formulating the Allies' strategic plans. Some of his ideas, like the floating harbors that he suggested for the D-Day invasion, were brilliant; others were clearly impractical, but he usually heeded his generals' advice on such matters.

In addition to his command role, Churchill's diplomatic skills proved invaluable in cementing Anglo-American relations, enabling him to secure the ships and armaments that Britain needed when it stood alone against Hitler and ensuring an unprecedented level of inter-Allied cooperation after the American entry into the war. Perhaps most important, by his words and his presence Winston Churchill was able to rally the British people and their Allies to the cause of victory even in the war's darkest days.

In July 1945—only two months after Churchill's hour of triumph on V-E Day—he was unseated in parliamentary elections, and thus no longer in office when the war against Japan finally ended. He was reelected prime minister in 1951, serving until 1955. Made a Knight of the Garter in 1954, he refused elevation to the peerage, not wanting to turn his back on the House of Commons. Sir Winston Churchill, England's man of the century, died in London on January 24, 1965, at the age of 90.

Churchill resigned from the army in 1899 to embark on a career as a politician and writer. In 1900, after covering the Boer War as a reporter (for which he gained national attention, particularly due to his daring escape from a Boer prisoner-of-war camp), he was elected to his first term in Parliament. Appointed First Lord of the Admiralty in 1912, he directed the Royal Navy's war preparations with great success, but after the failure of the Gallipoli campaign in 1915 he resigned to become lieutenant colonel of the Scots Fusiliers and saw combat in France.

In the postwar years Churchill held a variety of government positions. He argued unceasingly in Parliament for increased military preparedness and warned of the danger from Hitler's Germany, but his pleas went unheeded as Prime Minister Neville Chamberlain's government embarked on a campaign of appeasement. As a result, when war broke out following the invasion of Poland in September 1939, the British army was largely unprepared. In May 1940, as the British faced disaster, the ineffectual Chamberlain was ousted, and Churchill was selected to head a coalition government.

JOSEPH JOFFRE
France, 1852–1931

THROUGHOUT THE First World War, most of Germany's military strength was directed toward defeating France. The job of defending France against this German onslaught during the crucial first years of the war fell to the highly respected general lovingly known as "Papa"—Joseph Jacques Joffre.

Joffre was born in Riversaltes, France, on January 12, 1852. Following brief service in the Franco-Prussian War he graduated from the Ecole Polytechnique in Paris and enlisted in the army as an engineering officer in 1872. Joffre spent most of the next 30 years in French colonies in Africa and Indochina, rising to the rank of major general by 1905. Returning to France, he was appointed army chief of staff and vice president of the Conseil Supérieur de Guerre in 1911. While serving in this capacity he was instrumental in drafting Plan XVII, the secret French contingency plan for war with Germany.

When war was declared on August 3, 1914, General Joffre was assigned to the overall command of the French armies. In little more than a month he emerged as a national hero by directing the Allied counteroffensive at the First Battle of the Marne, which drove back the German invasion of France on September 5–10, 1914. Following this success, he promised "la guerre à l'outrance"—war to the bitter end—and embarked on the long, difficult campaign of trench warfare that characterized the fighting on the German front until the Armistice.

As the war dragged on into 1916, Papa Joffre's popularity declined. The German attack at Verdun, which he seriously underestimated, and the bloody stalemate at the Battle of the Somme, which lasted from July 1 to November 19 and resulted in some 200,000 French casualties cost Joffre his command. Promoted to marshal of France that December—the first man to hold the nation's highest military rank since 1870—Joffre was detailed to administrative duties in Paris and remained sidelined for the rest of the war. He was succeeded as commander in chief by Gen. Robert Nivelle.

After the war Marshal Joffre lived in relative obscurity, working on his mem-

Joseph Joffre, the steadfast commander of France's armies at the outset of World War I. On the chest of his marshal's uniform, he wears France's highest military decorations, the Medaille Militaire, and the Croix de Guerre.

DOUGLAS MacARTHUR
United States, 1880–1964

DOUGLAS MacARTHUR WAS arguably the most influential American military commander of the 20th century. As a brilliant strategist and organizer and a general officer for nearly 50 years, he made an immense contribution to the U.S. Army, one that earned him the sobriquet "the American Caesar."

(Opposite) An oil portrait of Gen. Douglas MacArthur in his trademark khaki uniform and cap. Brusque and egomaniacal, he was undeniably one of the finest military commanders in American history.

(Below) Supreme Allied Commander General MacArthur signing the Japanese treaty of surrender on board U.S.S. *Missouri*, September 2, 1945. Behind him stand U.S. Gen. Jonathan Wainwright and British Gen. Arthur Percival, both recently released from Japanese P.O.W. camps.

Douglas MacArthur was born in Little Rock, Arkansas, on January 26, 1880, the son of Arthur MacArthur II, a career officer. Douglas also opted for a career in the military, graduating first in his class from West Point in 1903 with a four-year record that remains unsurpassed there.

Commissioned a lieutenant in the elite Corps of Engineers, MacArthur served in the Philippines, the Far East, and as military aide to President Theodore Roosevelt. During the First World War, he became chief of staff of the famed 42nd Rainbow Division, earning 31 decorations for valor including the Distinguished Service Cross. In July 1918 he was upgraded to brigadier general, and subsequently named head of the Division's new 84th Brigade, which he led with distinction through the Marne

offensive in August and the Meuse-Argonne campaign two months later.

In the years between the wars, MacArthur served as Superintendent of West Point, Army Chief of Staff, U. S. commander in the Philippines, and top civilian adviser on military affairs to Filipino President Manuel Quezon. In July 1941, when war seemed imminent, he was recalled to active duty with the U.S. Army and given command of all the forces in the Philippines. Promoted to full general after Pearl Harbor, he directed the Allied defense of the islands against an overwhelming Japanese offensive which began on December 22. To avoid his capture, President Franklin D. Roosevelt ordered him to leave the Philippines for Australia, there to take charge of all Allied troops in the South

Pacific. Vowing "I shall return," he transferred command in March 1942 to his close friend Gen. Jonathan Wainwright. When Axis propaganda sought to brand him a coward for leaving, the American high command responded by awarding him the Congressional Medal of Honor for his heroic defense at Bataan and Corregidor.

In the months that followed, MacArthur directed a series of highly effective campaigns in the southwest Pacific that halted the Japanese advance and then threw them back. Finally, on October 19, 1944, he launched his historic return to the Philippines. Promoted to General of the Army that December, he directed U.S. land operations in the Pacific until the end of the war, when he accepted the Japanese surrender as the Allied Supreme Commander. In the ensuing years, he directed the postwar reconstruction of Japan, transforming the nation into a modern constitutional monarchy.

When the Korean War broke out in June 1950 MacArthur was named head of the United Nations troops that were mobilized to defend South Korea. That

September he launched one of the most audacious and brilliant attacks in military history, routing the North Korean army with a surprise amphibious landing in their rear at Inchon. However, the North's losses were reversed when the People's Republic of China began sending soldiers to their aid in November. MacArthur's plan to retaliate against China was vetoed by U.S. President Harry Truman, and after an acrimonious exchange the chief executive removed MacArthur from his commands in Korea and Japan on April 11, 1951.

MacArthur spent his final years in New York, where he served as chairman of Remington Rand, later Sperry-Rand. He died in Washington, D.C., on April 5, 1964.

(Right) MacArthur wading ashore at Lingayen Gulf in the Philippines on January 22, 1945. On reaching land he declared simply, "I have returned."

(Below) MacArthur addresses Congress on April 19,1951, after his removal as Supreme Allied Commander in Korea. "Old soldiers never die, they just fade away," he told the assemblage.

HEINZ GUDERIAN

Germany, 1888–1954

HEINZ GUDERIAN IS one of the 20th century's most innovative and influential military leaders. As head of Germany's armored (Panzer) forces during the Second World War he developed the Third Reich's concept of Blitzkrieg, or "lightning war," scoring unprecedented victories for Hitler in Poland, France, and Russia.

Guderian was born in Kulm, Prussia, on June 17, 1888. A graduate of the Royal Military Academy at Gross Lichterfelde, he served in the First World War as an infantry and staff officer on the western front. There, he became convinced of the importance of mechanized warfare after seeing the Allies' tanks in action breaking through the trench lines in 1917/18.

Guderian remained in the German army after the Armistice, slowly formulating his concept of Blitzkrieg and building the mobile communications systems and Panzer units that would make such a rapid war possible. His ideas greatly impressed Adolf Hitler, and after Hitler's rise to power in 1934 Guderian was promoted to brigadier general and appointed chief of staff of the Panzer Corps, which he continued to increase with the Furhrer's full support. Guderian became one of Hitler's most trusted subordinates, and on the eve of the Second World War in 1939 was named commander of the Third Reich's Panzer troops with the rank of general.

Guderian proved his theories of warfare to the world in Germany's Blitzkrieg invasion of Poland on September 1, 1939. Led by six Panzer divisions, the Nazi Army raced through Poland in a historic campaign that brought total victory to Germany in just 16 days. Transferred to the western theater of operations the following May General Guderian repeated his success in France, driving his Panzer group through the Ardennes Forest and across northern France to Calais in less than two weeks.

Guderian's most spectacular triumphs occurred during the German invasion of the USSR in 1941. In just six weeks he captured Brest-Litovsk and Minsk and advanced to within 200 miles of Moscow, halting only when he was ordered to support Gen. Gerd von Rundstedt's campaign against Kiev in August. Racing south, Guderian's Panzers played a key part in winning the greatest Nazi victory of the war on September 26 when more than half a million Soviet troops were encircled. He then returned to the advance on Moscow, only to be stopped by the severe winter weather and Gen. Georgi Zhukov's determined defense that December. Guderian felt that he could have captured the Soviet capital in August had he not been diverted to von Rundstedt's aid, and his anger over Hitler's bungling of the campaign caused him to be relieved of command on December 26. The general remained out of action until February 1943 when the German defeat at Stalingrad caused

the Fuehrer to name him inspector-general of Germany's Panzer troops. After the unsuccessful officers' coup against Hitler in July 1944 the dictator promoted Guderian, who was not involved, to head of the general staff. He served in that capacity until March 21, 1945, when the increasingly paranoid Fuehrer dismissed him for suggesting an armistice.

General Guderian was captured by advancing American forces on May 10, 1945. After his release he went into quiet retirement preparing his memoirs, which were published in 1951. The father of the Blitzkrieg died in Schwangau-bei-Füssen, West Germany, on May 15, 1954.

Gen. Heinz Guderian, innovative father of the Blitzkrieg, during the 1940 Nazi invasion of France.

GENERAL

MAXWELL TAYLOR
United States, 1901–1987

An oil portrait of Gen. Maxwell Taylor, the outstanding soldier and administrator whose distinguished career in the United States Army spanned the decades from World War II to Vietnam.

to Gen. Matthew Ridgway. Promoted to colonel, he was assigned with Ridgway to the 82nd Infantry Division, which they built into one of the army's first airborne units. Detailed to the Allied invasion of Sicily in July 1943, Brigadier General Taylor served as Ridgway's head of artillery.

Following the campaign for Sicily, General Taylor volunteered for one of the most dangerous espionage missions of the war. Sharing Ridgway's concern that an Allied air drop near Rome scheduled for September would be a disastrous mistake, he smuggled himself into the Italian capital and personally reconnoitered the situation. His reports enabled Ridgway to call off the ill-conceived assault and earned Taylor promotion to major general and command of the 101st Airborne Division. He subsequently led his command with distinction during the Normandy landing, the Battle of the Bulge, and the invasion of Germany.

After the war Taylor served as superintendent of West Point and Army Deputy Chief of Staff, rising to the rank of lieutenant general. Early in 1953 he assumed command of the Eighth Army in Korea, directing the final Allied assaults during the Korean conflict until the armistice was signed that July. Two years later, Taylor—by then a full general—succeeded his former commander Matthew Ridgway as Army Chief of Staff, retiring from the service at the end of his term in 1959. In 1961 President John F. Kennedy recalled him to duty as a special military adviser, and in September 1962 appointed him Chairman of the Joint Chiefs of Staff. While in office he was largely responsible for the massive commitment of United States forces in South Vietnam.

Taylor resigned from the army in 1965 when he was appointed U.S. Ambassador to South Vietnam by President Lyndon Johnson, but he continued to advise the administration on military matters until his retirement in 1969. He died in Washington, D.C., on April 19, 1987.

GEN. MAXWELL TAYLOR WAS one of the most influential American army officers of the mid-20th century. A pioneer of airborne tactics during the Second World War and an Allied commander in Korea, he eventually became Chairman of the Joint Chiefs of Staff, playing a crucial role in determining America's early involvement in Vietnam.

Maxwell Davenport Taylor was born in Keynesville, Missouri, on August 26, 1901. He entered West Point in 1918 and graduated near the top of his class four years later. Commissioned a lieutenant of engineers, he was transferred to a field artillery command in 1916, and by 1940 had reached the rank of major.

At the outbreak of the Second World War Taylor was serving as chief of staff

JOSEPH STALIN

USSR, 1879–1953

THE WARTIME ROLES of Joseph Stalin and Adolf Hitler contrast the greatest weaknesses and strengths of the two leaders. Both ruled their nations with absolute control and both directed their country's war efforts as supreme commander. Unlike Hitler, however, Stalin proved astute at high command, willing to trust the judgment of his best generals and learning from his mistakes.

Stalin was born in Gori, Georgia, on December 21, 1879, and christened Iosif Vissarionovich Dzhugashvili (he took the name Stalin—"man of steel"— around 1913). Although he was educated at an Orthodox seminary at Tbilisi, Stalin became a dedicated Marxist while in his teens, and by the time of the 1917 Russian Revolution he had risen to the highest levels of Lenin's Bolsheviks. During the Civil War that followed between 1918 and 1921 he proved himself as a Red Army commander at Petrograd (now Leningrad) and Tsaritsyn, later renamed Stalingrad in his honor. Following Lenin's death in 1924 Stalin embarked on a ruthless campaign for power which netted him total control of the Soviet government and the Communist Party by 1930. Late in the decade he purged the officer corps, "liquidating" many good commanders.

In August 1939 Stalin signed a nonaggression pact with Hitler's Reich, promising Soviet neutrality in the event of war in return for eastern Poland, the Baltic states, and other concessions. Believing that Hitler would stick to the agreement, Stalin was caught totally unprepared when the Wehrmacht struck on June 22, 1941. By the beginning of August Stalin recovered from his initial shock and took hold of the USSR's war machine, naming himself commissar of defense and supreme commander, with the rank of marshal. After some initial defeats (notably the loss of five entire armies at Kiev in September 1941) the Red Army under his top field commander, Marshal Georgi Zhukov, pushed the Germans back from Moscow that December and succeeded in stopping

(Left) A hand-tinted photo of Joseph Stalin taken in 1931, shortly after he had gained total control over the Soviet state.

(Opposite) Joseph Stalin (left), wearing the uniform of a marshal of the Russian army, with United States President Franklin Roosevelt (center) and British Prime Minister Winston Churchill during the "Big Three" conference at Tehran, Iran, in December 1943.

the Nazi advance across southern Russia in the six-month Battle of Stalingrad. By October 1943 Stalin's armies had taken much of the Russian territory acquired by Hitler, and by early 1945 they had advanced across Eastern Europe into Germany, capturing Berlin on May 2.

In addition to overseeing the USSR's campaigns in the field, Stalin also directed the vast industrial drive that produced a phenomenal output of tanks and warplanes. He also obtained substantial aid from the U.S. through "lend-lease."

A consummate negotiator, Stalin dealt ably with Prime Minister Winston Churchill and President Franklin D. Roosevelt, always pushing Soviet long-term goals. At the Yalta conference in February 1945, for example, he secured the postwar partition of Germany and

won major territorial concessions resulting in the subsequent Soviet domination of Eastern Europe.

After the war Stalin further solidified his position as ruler of the Soviet bloc through a series of bloody purges. He died in Moscow on March 5, 1953.

EDMUND ALLENBY

United Kingdom, 1861–1935

FIELD MARSHAL EDMUND ALLENBY compiled one of the most impressive records of any First World War commander. The general known as "the Bull" scored victories on both the European and Near Eastern fronts, ultimately engineering the defeat of the Central Powers' Turkish forces in the Near East.

Edmund Allenby was born at his grandfather's estate near Southwell, England, on April 23, 1861. Following his education at the Royal Military Academy at Sandhurst, Allenby, an accomplished horseman, was commissioned an officer in the Sixth Dragoons in 1882. He spent the next 32 years in the cavalry, rising to the rank of major general by 1909. At the beginning of the World War, General Allenby was appointed commander of the British army's cavalry forces in France. In recognition of his performance at the First Battle of Ypres in November, when he defended the center of the English line against heavy odds, the Bull was named head of the Fifth Corps, subsequently rising to command of the entire Third Army in October 1915.

Allenby's most outstanding accomplishment on the Western Front occurred at the Battle of Arras on April 9, 1917. His carefully planned assault drove the Germans back 3½ miles, the greatest single Allied advance made along the trench lines during the war. The determination and fighting spirit that earned the Bull his nickname made him a natural choice for commander of the Egyptian Expeditionary Force when the British war effort in the Near East stalled in 1917. Within weeks of his arrival at Cairo that June Allenby began turning things around, moving his headquarters to the front in Palestine and giving added support to Maj. T. E. Lawrence's guerrilla operations in Arabia. By November he had captured Gaza, and on December 11 he entered Jerusalem, ending 400 years of Turkish control over the holy city. General Allenby's campaign was interrupted by the transfer of many of his units to the European front during the early part of 1918, but by September of that year he was ready to resume operations against the Turks. In what was to be the final great cavalry campaign in modern warfare the Bull's troopers advanced 550

miles in 38 days, driving the Ottoman forces from Palestine. After securing Damascus on October 3 he continued pursuing the Turks northward, trapping them at Aleppo in northern Syria and forcing a Turkish surrender on October 30.

Following the Armistice, Allenby was promoted to field marshal and elevated to viscount. In March 1919, he was appointed British high commissioner for Egypt, a post that he held until 1925, when he returned to England. Field Marshal Lord Allenby died at his home in London on May 14, 1936, and is buried in Westminster Abbey.

(Opposite) Edmund Allenby, the victorious commander of the British forces in the Near East during World War I. His determined gaze and firmly-set jaw aptly reflect his nickname, "the Bull."

(Left) Field Marshal Allenby (left) with representatives of the Sultan of Egypt in Port Said. In 1921, when this photo was taken, Allenby was serving as British high commissioner.

MAULL & FOX
London.

HERMANN GOERING

Germany, 1893–1946

HERMANN GOERING WAS one of the key figures of the Third Reich. The second-ranking Nazi leader after Hitler, he engineered much of Germany's anti-Jewish legislation, and was most important to the war effort as commander of Germany's air force, the Luftwaffe.

Hermann Goering was born in Rosenheim, Prussia, on January 12, 1893, the son of a prominent judge. In 1911, Hermann graduated from the Royal Military Academy at Gross Lichterfelde, outside Berlin. At the beginning of the First World War he saw service as an infantry lieutenant but soon transferred to the air corps. During the war he scored 22 kills, earning the coveted Blue Max and promotion to the command of Manfred von Richthofen's Flying Circus in 1918 after that ace was killed.

In the years following the war Goering became one of Adolf Hitler's most devoted followers. The former war hero was named head of the Fuehrer's private army—the Brownshirts—in 1922 and took a leading role in the unsuccessful Beer Hall Putsch the next year, when he was badly wounded. After Hitler's appointment as Chancellor in 1933 Goering became commissioner for aviation and, in 1935, commander in chief of the newly established Luftwaffe.

By the opening days of the Second World War Goering had built the Luftwaffe into the largest air force in the world. His planes performed superbly in the Blitzkrieg campaigns against Poland, the Lowlands, and France, in recognition of which Goering was promoted to Reichsmarschall (a rank above field marshal) on June 19, 1940. Goering's hour of triumph was short-lived, however. He seriously mishandled the Battle of Britain in August and September, overestimating the Luftwaffe's capability for long-range combat and underestimating the resolve of Hugh Dowding's RAF. Goering's failure in Britain, which ended Hitler's dreams of a cross-Channel invasion, was compounded by his aviators' increasingly

This remarkably insightful portrait of Hermann Goering captures the malevolent intensity of Adolf Hitler's Luftwaffe commander.

poor performance during the Russian campaign in 1941. By early 1944 Allied bombers had turned the tide of the air war against Germany and Goering, unable to face the defeat of his Luftwaffe, retreated into a fantasy world fueled by his addiction to morphine.

Goering, who had been designated as Hitler's successor in 1939, was summarily dismissed and arrested on April 24, 1945, for suggesting that the Fuehrer resign in his favor. On May 9

the former Reichsmarschall was captured by soldiers of the U.S. Seventh Army. Subsequently tried and convicted of war crimes at Nuremberg, Hermann Goering committed suicide in his jail cell on October 15, 1946, two hours before he was to be hanged for his crimes against humanity.

Goering, marshal's baton in hand, reviewing Nazi troops. He reveled in the pomp of his office, changing uniforms as often as five times a day.

Goering first achieved fame as a pilot in World War I. Afterward, the future Luftwaffe commander became one of Germany's best-known stunt fliers.

FERDINAND FOCH

France, 1851–1929

MARSHAL FERDINAND FOCH was the most well liked and universally respected of all commanders in the First World War. A first-class offensive tactician and diplomat, he was the unanimous choice of the Western powers to serve as commander in chief of the Allied forces in Europe.

Foch was born at Tarbes, France, on October 2, 1851, the son of a minor government official. While serving as a private during the Franco-Prussian War in 1870 young Ferdinand decided upon a career in the military, and after graduating from the Ecole Polytechnique in 1873 he enlisted in the army as an artillery lieutenant. Foch became known as an effective offensive strategist and in 1894 was appointed professor of tactics in the Ecole Supérieur de Guerre with the rank of lieutenant colonel. There his reputation continued to climb, and after serving as chief of staff for the Fifth Army Corps he was promoted to brigadier general and made director of the Ecole in 1907.

At the onset of the Great War in August 1914 General Foch was assigned command of the 20th Army Corps. His unyielding advance at the Battle of Lorraine on August 14–20 marked him as a tenacious fighter, and in September he was promoted to division general in command of the Ninth Army. After driving back the Germans at the First Battle of the Marne on September 9, Foch was named one of General-in-Chief Joseph Joffre's deputies and assigned command of the entire northern sector of the Allied line.

In December 1916, with the front bogged down in bloody trench warfare, General Joffre was removed as commander of the French armies and Foch was dismissed with him. The latter's abilities were recognized as too important to France to be wasted, however, and when Philippe Pétain was named the new commanding general in May 1917 he appointed Foch his chief of staff.

With the arrival of Gen. John J. Pershing's American Expeditionary Force in Europe in the spring of 1918 it became obvious that a single commander in chief was needed to coordinate the Allied offensive against the Germans. General Foch, who had an excellent combat record and worked well with Pétain, Pershing, and British commander Field Marshal Sir Douglas Haig, was a natural choice. The former professor of field tactics—now promoted to marshal of France and generalissimo—skillfully directed the final Allied offen-

sives of the war, driving the German army from Château-Thierry to the Argonne until it no longer had the strength to fight. The victorious Foch then negotiated the Armistice agreement that ended the war at the 11th hour of the 11th day of the 11th month of 1918.

Following the Armistice Marshal Foch was hailed as one of France's greatest heroes. When he died in Paris on March 20, 1929 he was accorded a final honor—interment in the Invalides near the tomb of Napoleon.

Ferdinand Foch, the supreme Allied commander during World War I. An experienced solider and natural diplomat, Foch played a decisive role in coordinating French, British, and American efforts at the end of the war.

HENRY H. ARNOLD

United States, 1886–1950

Gen. Henry Arnold, the driving force behind the U.S. Army Air Force during World War II, in an oil portrait by Thomas E. Stephens.

DURING THE SECOND World War American air power played a decisive role in both Europe and the Pacific. The unprecedented success of the U.S. Army Air Forces in this conflict was due largely to the farsighted planning and skilled leadership of the AAF chief, Gen. Henry H. Arnold.

Henry Harley Arnold was born in Gladwyne, Pennsylvania, on June 25, 1886, the son of a local physician. In 1903 he entered the U.S. Military Academy, where his carefree attitude earned him his lifelong nickname, "Hap." Graduating in 1907, he was commissioned an infantry lieutenant and detailed to routine assignments in the Philippines and

New York. After four years of the mundane, Arnold was ready for a change, so he volunteered for the army's recently established Aeronautical Division. After two months of flight training with the Wright brothers he earned his wings in June 1911, becoming the first fully qualified pilot in the army. Designated U.S. Army Aviator Number 1, he proudly took up his next assignment—as instructor at the Aeronautical Division's first independent training camp.

When army aviation, now called the Air Service, was expanded during the First World War, Arnold's career rose meteorically. He was named deputy chief of aeronautics and promoted to colonel—at age 31 the youngest in the

army—but he was disappointed at receiving a desk job in Washington, D.C. When he finally managed a transfer to Europe in 1918 he caught pneumonia and did not make it to the front until after the Armistice.

During the 1920s Arnold served in California and Washington, D.C., where he supported his friend Billy Mitchell at the latter's 1925 court-martial. Six years later he was reassigned to California to organize a base at Camp March for bombers and pursuit (fighter) planes. His success there brought him promotion to brigadier general in 1935, and three years later he was named major general with command of the entire Army Air Corps.

As head of the Air Corps—later designated the Army Air Force in June 1941—Hap Arnold played a decisive role in preparing the United States for entry into the Second World War. Working closely with Army Chief of Staff George C. Marshall, he coordinated the recruitment of fliers and the increased production of aircraft that made an American air war possible. After Pearl Harbor he became one of the chief architects of Allied victory, directing AAF strategy in both the Pacific and European theaters of operations and serving as President Roosevelt's top adviser on the war for the skies.

Although his relentless schedule of conferences and visits to the front caused Arnold to suffer a heart attack in 1943, he refused to slow his pace and remained in command throughout the conflict. In recognition of his tremendous contribution to the war effort he was named one of the country's first Generals of the Army in December 1944 along with Douglas MacArthur, Dwight D. Eisenhower, and George C. Marshall.

Hap Arnold stepped down from active duty in 1946 and retired to his home near Sonoma, California. He died there on January 15, 1950, and was buried at Arlington National Cemetery.

JONATHAN WAINWRIGHT

United States, 1883–1953

ALTHOUGH Douglas MacArthur is rightfully honored as the liberator of the Philippines, in many ways the true hero of the struggle for that island nation was Gen. Jonathan Wainwright, who mounted a determined defense against overwhelming odds and became in the process an inspiration for Allied fighting men the world over.

Jonathan Mayhew Wainwright IV was born at an army post in Walla Walla, Washington, on August 23, 1883. Following in his father's footsteps, he entered the U.S. Military Academy in 1902, graduating as Cadet First Captain in 1906. Commissioned a lieutenant of cavalry, he distinguished himself as a staff officer in the 82nd "All American" Division during the First World War and rose to the rank of lieutenant colonel.

After the war he was named to the General Staff in Washington, D.C., where he helped prepare contingency plans for defense of the Philippines. Following studies at the Army War College and Command School, he was promoted to colonel and appointed commander of the Third Cavalry in 1936, a prestigious assignment that led to a brigadier general's commission three years later.

When the southward Japanese thrust in the Pacific became a clear-cut threat to the Philippines in 1940, General Wainwright was promoted to major general and given command of the forces on the island of Luzon north of Manila, the key area where the Japanese launched their invasion on December 22, 1941. Unable to stop the enemy advance, Wainwright, with permission of his commander, Gen. Douglas MacArthur, withdrew to a fallback position west of Manila, on the southern peninsula of Bataan. When MacArthur was ordered to Australia on March 11, Wainwright succeeded to command of the American forces in the Philippines with the rank of lieutenant general. He continued to hold his position on Bataan until April 9, but when his forces could clearly no longer withstand the Japanese onslaught, Wainwright managed to shift 13,000 Allied soldiers and hospital personnel to the island fortress of Corregidor in Manila Bay. There his inspiring leadership carried the defenders through a month of nonstop shelling. Finally, facing utter annihilation, he was

granted permission to capitulate by President Roosevelt, and on May 6 he surrendered all of the American troops in the Philippines.

Wainwright was held in prisoner-of-war camps until August 24, 1945. Upon his release, he feared that he would be court-martialed for his defeat three years earlier; instead he was given a place of honor at the Japanese surrender on the U.S.S. *Missouri* on September 2. His return to America thereafter was greeted with parades, a promotion to full general, and presentation of the Congressional Medal of Honor by President Truman. Wainwright retired from the service in 1947 and died in San Antonio, Texas, on September 2, 1953.

(Below) Jonathan Wainwright in a photo taken just prior to World War II when the hero of Corregidor was a self-assured brigadier general.

(Opposite) Douglas MacArthur embraces a gaunt Wainwright at their first meeting after the latter's release from three years of captivity in a Japanese P.O.W. camp.

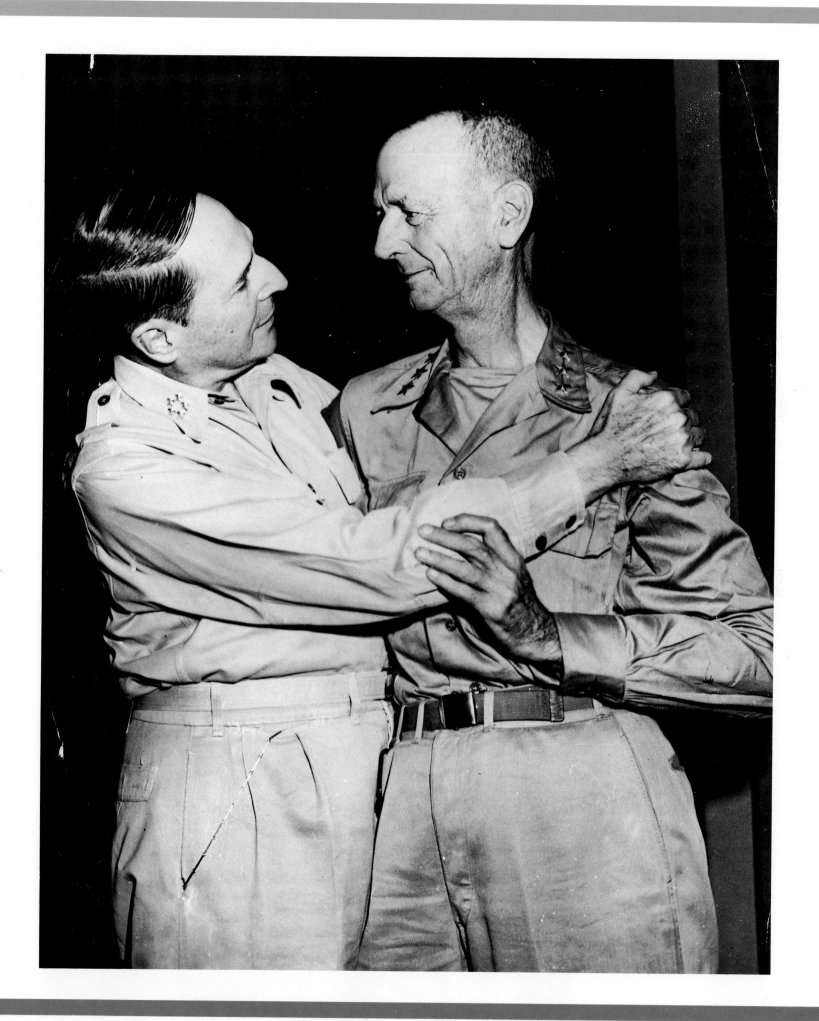

HEIHACHIRO TOGO

Japan, 1848–1934

ON MAY 27, 1905, the Russo-Japanese War was climaxed by the largest naval engagement in history, the Battle of Tsushima. The decisive Japanese victory in this battle was masterminded by one of the ablest naval officers of his time, Fleet Adm. Heihachiro Togo.

Togo was born in Kagoshima, Japan, in 1848, the descendant of an old samurai family. The future admiral received his baptism of fire as a boy of 15 when he helped man the defenses of Kagoshima against an attack by British warships on August 15, 1863. Impressed by this demonstration of maritime strength, Togo enlisted in the navy of the Satsuma domain as soon as he graduated from school. The young ensign quickly proved himself a talented officer and after the Meiji Restoration in 1871 was selected by the Japanese government to study naval tactics in Britain. Upon his return to Japan in 1878 he was commissioned a lieutenant in the Imperial Navy, and by 1903 had risen to the rank of vice admiral.

When Japanese plans for the war against Russia were being formulated in 1903, Admiral Togo was personally selected by the Meiji Emperor to command the fleet that would open the fighting. On February 8, 1904, in a sneak attack presaging the one on Pearl Harbor 40 years later, Togo's ships opened fire on the Russian naval base at Port Arthur, China, crippling much of the Russian Pacific squadron. Togo then instituted a blockade of the port that successfully kept the fleet bottled up until the city's surrender on January 2, 1905. The only serious Russian attempt to outrun Togo's warships ended in disaster when the Japanese sank the Russian commander's flagship at the Battle of the Yellow Sea on August 10, 1904.

Faced with defeat and the loss of its Pacific fleet, the Russian High Command ordered its Baltic squadron to the relief of Port Arthur on October 15,

1904. After steaming halfway around the world, the Russian fleet of 33 battleships, cruisers, and destroyers arrived at the Straits of Tsushima between Japan and Korea in early May 1905. But, when the Russians moved against Admiral Togo's armada of 33 warships and 60 torpedo boats on May 27, the Japanese commander was ready. In a brilliant display of naval tactics he positioned his ships ahead of the Tsarist fleet and unleashed a devastating bombardment that destroyed two battleships in less than two hours. He then proceeded to encircle the remaining Russian vessels and by the following afternoon had all but annihilated his

foe. Only three small Russian ships managed to escape; the Japanese, by contrast, had lost only three torpedo boats.

Admiral Togo's unparalleled victory at Port Arthur made him a national hero, the emperor made him a baron, and he was decorated by several nations in addition to his own. Although he retired from active duty at the close of the war, Togo continued to serve as military adviser to the emperor and was promoted to fleet admiral in 1913. After many years of government service, Lord Togo died at his home in Yasakuni, Japan, on May 31, 1934.

Adm. Heihachiro Togo, commander in chief of the Japanese navy during the Russo-Japanese War. His decisive victory at the Battle of Tsushima has earned him a place among the outstanding naval officers of all time.

FOR SEVERAL MONTHS following the fall of France in June 1940 the fate of Britain hung by a slender thread. Under constant attack by Hitler's Luftwaffe, only the fabled "few"—the fighter pilots of the Royal Air Force—stood between England and German invasion. The victory of these aviators in the Battle of Britain was largely due to the inspired leadership of their commander, the RAF's Air Chief Marshal, Hugh Dowding.

Hugh Caswall Tremenheere Dowding was born in Moffat, Scotland, on April 24, 1882. Like Winston Churchill, he had difficulty with the classical subjects taught at British "public" (that is, prep) schools, so he opted for a military education. Upon his graduation from the Royal Military Academy at Woolwich he was commissioned an artillery officer, but after several years he decided to enter the aeronautical service instead. The future air marshal earned his wings in 1913 and was subsequently transferred to the Royal Flying Corps, the forerunner of the RAF.

During the Great War Dowding served as a squadron and wing commander in France, rising to the rank of brigadier general. In the years following the Armistice he emerged as one of the RAF's finest strategic planners and in 1930 was appointed to the Air Council as head of research and supply. The innovative airman championed the development of the Hurricane and Spitfire fighter planes and the creation of Britain's radar and ground-to-air communications systems, all of which would later prove crucial to the defense of the island.

In the summer of 1936 Dowding was made head of the RAF Fighter Command and the following year was promoted to the rank of air chief marshal. He worked tirelessly to build Britain's air defenses for the showdown that loomed with the German Luftwaffe. The Battle of Britain, the fight for control of the island's skies, began in earnest on August 13, 1940, with a series of raids on the English heartland by Nazi fighters and bombers. Although the RAF's 1,200 fighters were badly outnumbered by the Luftwaffe's 2,500 aircraft, Dowding's extensive radar and radio systems allowed him to anticipate the German attacks and concentrate his planes where they were most needed, effectively neutralizing the Nazis' numerical

Lord Hugh Dowding, the farsighted planner who led the Royal Air Force to its decisive victory in the Battle of Britain.

advantage. In addition, British escalation of aircraft production in secret "shadow factories" during the battle enabled Dowding to replace lost planes in a way that the Germans simply could not equal. By mid-September the RAF had made the fighting over England so costly to the Luftwaffe that Reichsmarschall Hermann Goering was forced to abandon the campaign, marking the end of Hitler's plans for the invasion of Britain.

Unfortunately, Air Chief Marshal Dowding did not savor his triumph for long. Well over the RAF's mandatory retirement age, he was knighted that September, then abruptly removed from command on November 25, and sent on a tour of North America. In 1943 he was elevated to Baron Dowding of Bentley Priory. The victor of the Battle of Britain died at his home in Tunbridge Wells, England, on February 15, 1970, and was given a hero's burial in Westminster Abbey.

DWIGHT D. EISENHOWER

United States, 1890–1969

IN AN ARMY DOMINATED by colorful commanders like Douglas MacArthur and George S. Patton, Gen. Dwight D. Eisenhower seemed an unlikely candidate to rise to top command during the Second World War. Soft-spoken and without prior combat experience, "Ike" nevertheless possessed remarkable gifts for leadership and strategic planning, and these skills made him what many regard as the war's greatest master of high command.

Dwight David Eisenhower was born in Denison, Texas, on October 14, 1890,

and raised in Abilene, Kansas. As his father was unable to pay for his college education Dwight applied to the U.S. Military Academy, upsetting his mother, who was a pacifist. Graduating in the top half of his class in 1915, Ike was commissioned an officer in the infantry and posted to Texas. During the First World War he commanded a tank training camp near Gettysburg, Pennsylvania, and although he rose to the rank of lieutenant colonel he was greatly disappointed at not receiving a combat command in France.

In the 1920s and 1930s Eisenhower held a variety of staff positions including

(Opposite) An oil portrait of one of the of the greatest military leaders to emerge from World War II, Gen. of the Army Dwight D. Eisenhower, wearing the waist-length "Ike" jacket he popularized.

(Below) Ike chats with members of the U.S. Army Rangers a few hours before launching the D-Day invasion. Eisenhower often went out of his way to meet with his troops, preferring this personal approach to Patton-esque pep talks.

Eisenhower gives the victory sign on election night in 1952, when the immensely popular general became the first Republican president in 20 years.

four years as Gen. Douglas MacArthur's chief of staff in the Philippines. The two men did not get along, however, and in 1940 Eisenhower returned to the United States. The following year he gained appointment as chief of staff of the Third Army and was promoted to brigadier general.

When the United States entered the Second World War in December 1941 General Eisenhower was assigned to Washington, D.C., to help with mobilization in the Operations Division of the War Department. His thoroughly professional approach impressed Army Chief of Staff George C. Marshall, who engineered Ike's rapid promotions to lieutenant general, and his appointment as commander of U.S. forces in Britain in July 1942. Shortly after arriving overseas, General Eisenhower was given his first combat role as commander of "Operation Torch," the Allied invasion of North Africa that November. His success in coordinating the landings in Morocco and Algeria with the British offensive under Gen. Bernard Montgomery's operations in Libya and Tunisia won him promotion to full general and command of the Allied invasion of Italy in May 1943.

The victories scored by Ike's Anglo-American task force at Sicily in July and in southern Italy the following fall further demonstrated his skill at both strategic planning and inter-Allied diplomacy and made him the natural choice for supreme commander of the Allied invasion of Normandy set for the following June. As head of "Operation Overlord"—the code name for the invasion—General Eisenhower played a

crucial role in its success, determining the number and types of troops to be deployed, overseeing their training, and arranging for essential naval and air support for the landings. His bold decision to launch the attack in poor weather on June 6, 1944, greatly added to the surprise which made the assault a success. Following the landings Eisenhower commanded all Allied forces in Europe, prosecuting the war against the Third Reich to its conclusion and earning promotion to the five-star rank, general of the army.

After the war General Eisenhower served as Army Chief of Staff and supreme NATO commander. In 1952 he was elected President of the United States. After eight years as chief executive, he retired to his farm in Gettysburg, Pennsylvania. Dwight Eisenhower died in Washington, D.C., on March 18, 1969, and was buried near his boyhood home in Abilene.

ERICH LUDENDORFF
Germany, 1865–1937

ALTHOUGH FIELD MARSHAL Paul von Hindenburg was the nominal commander in chief of the German forces during most of the First World War, the actual driving force behind the Kaiser's armies was Hindenburg's chief of staff, Gen. Erich Ludendorff. Ruthless and manipulative, Ludendorff gradually gained control over his nation's armies and government until, in the last years of the war, he was virtually running Germany.

Erich Friedrich Wilhelm Ludendorff was born in Kruschevnia, Prussia, (now Poland) on April 9, 1865. He began his military training as a boy in the cadet school at Plon, moving up to the Royal Military Academy at Gross Lichterfelde in 1880. At the conclusion of his studies in 1885 Ludendorff was commissioned a lieutenant in the 57th Infantry, but his precise attention to detail quickly earned him appointment as a staff officer. By 1907 he had risen to the rank of lieutenant colonel on the Imperial General Staff, where he played a key role in formulating Germany's plans for war.

When the long-anticipated conflict began in August 1914 Colonel Ludendorff coordinated the German capture of Liège, Belgium, winning Germany's highest decoration, the Pour le Mérite for his efforts. Following this victory, he was assigned as chief of staff to Paul von Hindenburg on the Russian front, where he catapulted Hindenburg to fame by planning the brilliant German victories at the Battles of Tannenberg and the Masurian Lakes.

When Field Marshal von Hindenburg was named commander in chief of the Kaiser's forces in August 1916 Ludendorff remained his closest adviser, becoming the de facto director of Germany's war effort. Promoted to quartermaster general, he used the authority of his new office—the supervision of military supply production—to gain control over the entire German economy. By 1917 his influence with Hindenburg and with the Kaiser was so great that he engineered the ouster of the moderate Chancellor Theobald von Bethmann-Hollweg and effectively gained control of the government as well.

Ludendorff's power waned with Ger-

late 1917 and 1918. These losses were largely due to the general's overextension of resources and his support of unlimited submarine warfare, the latter having brought the United States into the war. The Allied assault which shattered the German lines near Amiens on August 8, 1918—"the Black Day of the German Army" as Ludendorff labeled it—brought the general's days of glory to a swift end. Realizing that Germany could not possibly win the war, he urged the Kaiser to seek an armistice

Gen. Erich Ludendorff, the controversial Germany army chief of staff during World War I. His waxed moustache, closely cropped hair, and militaristic bearing made him seem the living embodiment of Allied caricatures of the enemy.

and then went on an extended leave of absence, finally tendering his resignation from the army on October 26. By the Armistice, with Berlin in chaos, he was forced to don a disguise and flee for his life.

In the years following the war Ludendorff, like many other embittered German nationalists, became an active supporter of Adolf Hitler's Nazi Party. In 1923 he took part in the abortive Beer Hall Putsch, and two years later ran for president of Germany on the Nazi ticket. After Hitler's rise to power Ludendorff was again hailed as a national hero and was offered the post of field marshal, which he declined. General Ludendorff died in Munich on December 20, 1937.

DOUGLAS HAIG

United Kingdom, 1861–1928

SEVENTY YEARS AFTER the end of the First World War, Field Marshal Lord Douglas Haig remains one of the conflict's most controversial commanders. The man who led the British Expeditionary Force to victory in the Great War has been condemned by some as callous and unimaginative and hailed by others—among them Winston Churchill—as one of the greatest British generals in history.

Born in Edinburgh, Scotland, on June 19, 1861, Douglas Haig attended Oxford University for three years before entering the Royal Military College at Sandhurst in 1883. Upon his graduation at the top of his class the following year, Haig was commissioned an officer in the Seventh Hussars and detailed to India. Popular and intelligent, he rapidly rose to prominence, and after service in the Boer War he was appointed a major general of cavalry in 1904 by Lord Kitchener. Haig's subsequent service on the Imperial General Staff led to his being named a Knight Commander of the Victorian Order in 1909 and promoted to lieutenant general the following year.

At the onset of the Great War General Haig was assigned to lead the British First Army Corps in France. His determined defense of the Allied left at the First Battle of Ypres from October 19 to November 22, 1914, brought him to national prominence and earned him command of the entire First Army that December. Haig's capability for high command was soon demonstrated at the Battle of Neuve-Chapelle on March 10–13, 1915. In what became the model plan for offensive trench warfare, Sir Douglas heavily bombarded the German lines with artillery and then rapidly sent in his infantry to capture the weakened positions before reinforcements could make their way forward.

Field Marshal Douglas Haig, the hard-hitting commander of the British Expeditionary Force during the final years of World War I.

Haig (center left) and Marshal Foch inspect an honor guard of Scottish troops a few days after the Armistice. The two leaders developed an excellent working relationship during the war.

Haig's success at Neuve-Chapelle marked him as one of the British Expeditionary Force's top generals, and he was appointed the BEF's commander in chief in December with promotion to field marshal coming a year later. Stalemated on the trench lines, Haig entered into a bloody war of attrition with the Germans which he described as one continuous battle. Although the fighting earned him a reputation as a commander unconcerned about his soldiers' lives Haig's dogged tactics, like those of Ulysses S. Grant in the U.S. Civil War, **ultimately proved successful and ended a struggle which might otherwise have lasted another two years with the loss of thousands more.**

Following the allied victory Field Marshal Haig was elevated to earl and named commander in chief of the British home forces. Upon his retirement from the army in 1921 he spent his remaining years helping the veterans of the Great War. Field Marshal Lord Haig died in London on January 30, 1928, and is buried near his ances-

ADOLF HITLER
Germany, 1889–1945

ADOLF HITLER WAS the central figure of the Second World War. The leader (Fuehrer) of the Third Reich, he also made himself commander in chief of the Nazi war machine. The former First World War corporal considered himself a brilliant military strategist and constantly interfered in his generals' war plans, ignoring their advice and embarking on a series of audacious campaigns that were at first successful but ultimately led to the Third Reich's crushing defeat.

Adolf Hitler was born in Braunau-am-Inn on the Austro-Bavarian border, on April 20, 1889, the son of a minor Austrian customs official. As a youth Hitler displayed little interest in schoolwork, hoping to become an artist. Rejected by the Austrian Academy of Fine Arts in 1907, he spent several years in Vienna, where he made a meager living peddling his watercolors in the streets. He also developed an avid interest in right-wing politics.

At the outbreak of the First World War Hitler enlisted in the German army, earning the Iron Cross for bravery on the western front as a corporal in the 16th Bavarian Infantry. After the Armistice he stayed on in the army as a political liaison and undercover informer in Munich, where he became active in the National Socialist German Workers (Nazi) Party. A remarkably persuasive speaker, Hitler soon took over the post of party chairman and initiated an ill-fated effort to overthrow the Bavarian government in the Beer Hall Putsch of November 1923. Arrested for his role in the attempted coup, he spent the next year in prison, using the time to write *Mein Kampf* ("My Struggle"), a manifesto of his political beliefs.

With the coming of the Depression the Nazi Party gained tremendous support in Germany, and Hitler rapidly rose to national prominence. In 1933 the aging president of Germany, Paul von Hindenburg, appointed Hitler chancellor. On Hindenburg's death the following year Hitler eliminated the office of president and named himself Fuehrer of the German people, ruthlessly silencing any opposition through the use of his secret police—the Gestapo—and his persecution of Jews and other "enemies of the state." Hitler immediately proceeded to rebuild Germany as an international

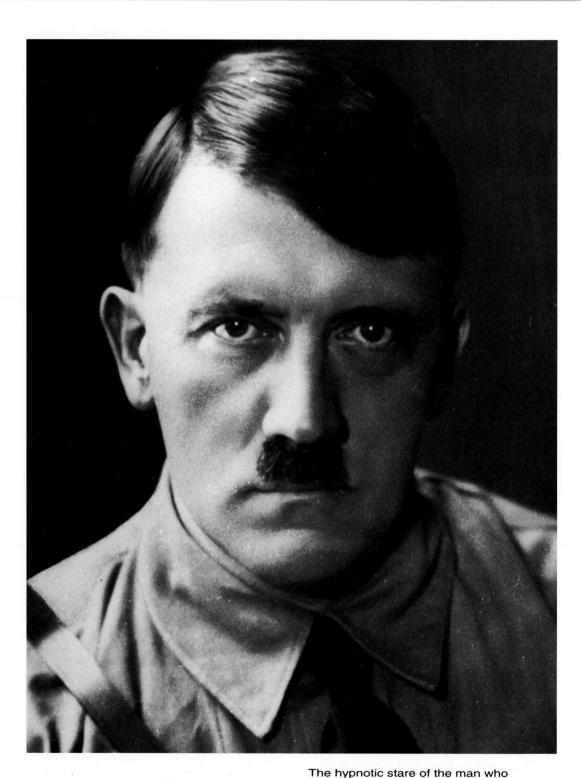

The hypnotic stare of the man who plunged the world into war—German Reichsfuehrer Adolf Hitler.

The Fuehrer reviews plans with his foreign minister Joachim von Ribbentrop. Hitler attemped to control every aspect of the administration of his Third Reich—including its war effort—with disastrous results.

Hitler enters one of the carefully choreographed Nazi Party rallies which were mainstays of political life in the Third Reich.

annexed Austria and later the Sudeten-land and northern Czechoslovakia.

Hitler, who had declared himself com-mander in chief of the German armed forces (*Wehrmacht*) in 1938, soon plunged Europe into the Second World War with his Blitzkrieg invasion of Poland in September 1939. His later stunning successes in Scandinavia, the Low Countries, and France reinforced his self-image as a brilliant military strategist, and he became an increasing impediment to general staff planning, refusing both criticism and advice from his high command. After the Luftwaffe failed to destroy the RAF over Britain, he overran Yugoslavia and Greece, then launched the disastrous invasion of the USSR in June 1941.

Germany's heavy losses in 1943 and 1944 made Hitler ever more distrustful of his commanders. His orders grew increasingly irrational, and he began to push for the development of "miracle weapons" like V-rockets and jet planes to win the war. A group of high-ranking officers unsuccessfully staged an assassination attempt against him on July 20, 1944. After this, the Fuehrer isolated himself from all but his closest lieutenants, dismissing even them in his last days. Facing imminent defeat, his "thousand-year Reich" in ruins, Adolf Hitler committed suicide at his underground headquarters in Berlin on April 30, 1945.

Hitler and his trusted air marshal Hermann Goering acknowledge the cheers of the crowd. A master manipulator, the Fuehrer inspired fanatical displays of support from his followers.

GEORGE C. MARSHALL

United States, 1880–1959

UNLIKE MANY OF the generals in this book whose primary contributions came from their ability to lead men in battle, it was George Marshall's incomparable skill as a master planner that made him one of the Allies' most important commanders during the Second World War. It also earned him promotion to five-star general, the highest rank in the American army.

George Catlett Marshall, Jr. was born in Uniontown, Pennsylvania, on December 31, 1880. A graduate of the Virginia Military Academy in 1901, Marshall was commissioned a lieutenant in the U.S. Army the following year and assigned to duty in the western United States and the Philippines. It was there that he first distinguished himself as a staff officer.

Upon America's entry into the First World War Marshall, by then a captain, was assigned as chief of operations to the First Infantry Division in France. His meticulous work so impressed American commander Gen. John Pershing that he named Marshall his principal aide, a position that he retained until Pershing's retirement in 1924. Marshall subsequently served with U.S. troops in China, then as assistant commandant of the infantry school at Fort Benning, Georgia, and later as commander of the Fifth Infantry Brigade in the state of Washington, rising to the rank of brigadier general in 1936. However, General Marshall did not remain with the Fifth Infantry for long. In 1938 he was transferred to Washington, D.C., as head of the army's war plans division and Deputy Chief of Staff. President Franklin D. Roosevelt promoted him to Chief of Staff with the rank of full general on the day that war broke out in Europe—September 1, 1939—and Marshall immediately began building up American defenses. He increased the U.S. Army to the maximum peacetime strength allowed by law, upgraded training, and helped the president secure additional funding from Congress. Under Marshall's careful guidance, when the United States entered World War II in December 1941 it was better prepared than it had been for any previous conflict.

For the duration of the war General Marshall directed the American war effort at home and abroad, overseeing the production and distribution of material and the deployment of an army of eight million men and women. He also served as President Roosevelt's closest military adviser, playing a key role in establishing overall strategies and selecting Allied commanders.

General Marshall laid much of the groundwork for the D-Day invasion and was slated to serve as Supreme Allied Commander of Operation Overlord—as the cross-Channel invasion was called—until the president decided that he could not be spared from his duties in Washington even for that campaign. Thus Marshall remained as Chief of Staff until the end of the war, when his immense contribution to the Allied cause was recognized by his promotion to general of the army on December 16, 1945. Retiring from active duty, Marshall subsequently served as secretary of state and secretary of defense in the Truman administration. The famous Marshall Plan for postwar European economic recovery earned him the Nobel Peace Prize in 1953. George C. Marshall died in Washington, D.C., on October 16, 1959, and is buried in a place of honor in Arlington National Cemetery.

(Opposite) George C. Marshall, the invaluable U.S. Army Chief of Staff during World War II, in a 1949 oil painting by James Anthony Wills.

(Below) Marshall (left) on a wartime tour of Army installations on Oahu, Hawaii. He seldom left Washington except for major Allied conferences because President Franklin Roosevelt depended so heavily on his advice. "I didn't feel I could sleep at ease if [Marshall was] out of Washington," FDR once confessed.

ALFRED VON TIRPITZ
Germany, 1849–1930

THE IMPERIAL GERMAN masterplan for the First World War called for an extensive naval war as well as a two-front land campaign in Europe. The man who made the Kaiser's maritime plans possible was Alfred von Tirpitz, Germany's first grand admiral and one of the most influential figures in modern maritime history.

Alfred Peter Fredrich von Tirpitz was born in Kustrin, Prussia, on March 19, 1849. He enlisted in the Prussian navy as a junior officer at the age of 16 in 1865. Advancing quickly, he became head of the navy's torpedo boat squadron before he was 30, developing it into a major offensive force he called his "black host." Following service as naval chief of staff and as commander of the German squadron in the Far East, von Tirpitz was promoted to rear admiral in 1895 and named navy state secretary two years later.

As head of the Navy Department Admiral von Tirpitz engineered one of the most massive buildups of maritime might in modern history, overseeing the construction of a fleet of more than 50 battleships and cruisers, an armada that offered the first serious challenge to British naval superiority since Napoleon. The creation of this force, which he referred to as a "gleaming dagger" aimed at Britain, earned von Tirpitz elevation to the Prussian house of lords in 1908 and promotion to the rank of grand admiral, Germany's first, in 1911.

With the onset of the Great War in 1914 von Tirpitz's shipbuilding campaign was put on hold while the German war effort shifted to the Kaiser's land forces. The defeat of Adm. Maximilian von Spee's Far Eastern fleet on December 11, 1914, signaled the end of the grand admiral's dream of developing an all-powerful naval armada. Denied government support for replacing lost ships, von Tirpitz resigned from the navy in disgust on March 15, 1916, shortly before the Battle of Jutland, which effectively ended the threat of his highly vaunted battle fleet to Britain. Following this costly blunder, the Kaiser's government concentrated its naval efforts on submarines rather than battleships, with the ultimately fatal result of provoking American entry into the war in 1917.

During his retirement Alfred von Tirpitz entered politics, serving in the German Parliament from 1924 to 1928. He died in Ebenhausen, Germany, on March 6, 1930. In the years that followed he was hailed by Hitler as the father of the German Navy, and the Third Reich's largest battleship was named *Tirpitz* in his honor.

Grand Adm. Alfred von Tirpitz, father of the modern German Navy and master planner of German naval operations during World War I.

ISOROKU YAMAMOTO

Japan, 1884–1943

THE JAPANESE NAVY'S devastating surprise attack on the U.S. naval base at Pearl Harbor, Hawaii, is arguably the single most consequential military event of the 20th century. The flawlessly executed plan was the creation of Japan's preeminent naval officer of the war, Adm. Isoroku Yamamoto.

Yamamoto was born in Nagaoka, Japan, on April 4, 1884. Originally named Isoroku Takano, he took the surname Yamamoto after he was adopted by a prestigious local family of that name when his parents died. Yamamoto entered the Imperial Naval Academy in 1900, graduating four years later as an ensign. His bravery under fire during the Battle of Tsushima the following year marked him as one of the navy's most promising young officers, and he was subsequently promoted and sent for advanced training to the Japanese Naval War College and to Harvard University.

During his years in the West Yamamoto became convinced of the strategic importance of carrier-based aircraft, which were then being developed by the United States and Britain. After his return to Japan he was placed in charge of the fledgling naval air arm, which he built into the world-class carrier force that played such a crucial role during the Pacific war. In recognition of his accomplishments he was promoted to rear admiral in 1931, and five years later was named vice-minister of the Imperial Navy.

As Japan became embroiled in its war with China in the late 1930s, Yamamoto stood alone among the imperial high command in urging caution, believing that a clash with the United States would only result in defeat. Nonetheless, the government promoted him in 1939 to commander in chief of the navy with the rank of admiral, secure in the knowledge that his code of honor bound him to fight aggressively despite his personal misgivings. This assessment was borne out on December 7, 1941, when 363 planes from Yamamoto's carriers destroyed most of the U.S. Pacific Fleet.

In the months that followed, Admiral Yamamoto led his forces to additional victories against the Dutch at Java and the British in Ceylon. But his advantage in the Pacific was nullified by his major

Midway in June 1942 and at Guadalcanal in November. On April 18, 1943, while on a tour of naval installations in the Solomon Islands, his plane was shot down by American fighter pilots over Bougainville. His loss was mourned throughout Japan, and he was posthumously promoted to fleet admiral.

Adm. Isoroku Yamamoto, the brilliant naval strategist who masterminded the devastating Japanese sneak attack on Pearl Harbor.

HORATIO KITCHENER

United Kingdom, 1850–1916

FIELD MARSHAL Earl Kitchener of Khartoum is one of the most highly respected commanders in British history. The commander who led the United Kingdom to victory in the Boer War and was the architect of Britain's war effort during the First World War had an outstanding record of service that was limited only by his untimely death in 1916.

Horatio Herbert Kitchener was born in Ballylongford, Ireland, on June 24, 1850, the son of Lt. Col. Henry Kitchener. Following his initial schooling in Switzerland, Horatio was admitted to the Royal Military Academy at Woolwich, England, in 1868. Commissioned an officer in the Royal Engineers in 1871, he spent most of the next 28 years at posts in Africa, rising to the rank of major general. For his part in commanding the British forces against the fanatic Mahdists in Sudan's River War in 1898 he was given the title Baron Kitchener of Khartoum, and later elevated to earl.

During the Boer War, which broke out in South Africa in 1899, General Kitchener was assigned as chief of staff to the British commander, Lord Roberts. While Gen. Sir Redvers Buller handled operations in the eastern theater of operations, Kitchener served as Roberts' second in command in the western theater, spearheading the British advance on Pretoria. When Roberts returned to England in November 1900 Lord Kitchener succeeded him as commander in chief. In this capacity he directed the British campaign against Louis Botha's guerrillas, establishing a network of blockhouses across central South Africa which successfully halted the Boer's commando raids and forced an end to the war in 1902. In recognition of his outstanding service Kitchener was made commander of the British troops in India and promoted to field marshal.

Lord Horatio Kitchener as he appeared during the Boer War, the very model of a proper British officer.

At the onset of the First World War in 1914 Lord Kitchener was appointed secretary of state for war and placed in charge of organizing the British war effort. Unlike most of his contemporaries he recognized that the struggle would be long and costly, and accordingly instituted a massive recruiting drive. The almost 2.5 million troops raised through this effort supplied the manpower that enabled Britain to carry on the war to victory. In addition to overseeing the mobilization and supply of his armies Lord Kitchener also directed strategic planning in the crucial first year of the war, coordinating the British campaigns from France to the Near East with great skill. In appreciation for his untiring efforts he was made a Knight of the Garter, Britain's highest order, in June 1915.

Lord Kitchener died in the line of duty on June 5, 1916, en route to a conference with the Russian high command, when his cruiser H.M.S. *Hampshire* hit a mine and sank off the Orkneys. Many believe that, had he survived, the war might have ended a year earlier than it did.

Kitchener (left), at 65, clearly shows his age while touring the front at Gallipoli, Turkey, in November 1915. The field marshal traveled extensively during the war, a practice that ultimately led to his death in 1916 when his ship was sunk by a German U-boat.

U.S. pilots in China—members of Gen. Claire Chennault's celebrated "Fighting Tigers"—make a dash for their fighter planes in order to give chase to the Japanese during a World War II air raid.

FIGHTING MEN

AUDIE MURPHY

United States, 1924–1971

THE SECOND WORLD WAR, like most wars, was a young man's struggle. It was not unusual for officers and NCOs in their thirties to be addressed as "Pappy" or "Grandpa" by recruits still in their teens. It is therefore fitting that the United States' most highly-decorated hero during the Second World War was not some battle-scarred veteran of the Great War but a 21-year-old boy named Audie Murphy.

Murphy was born on June 20, 1924, near Kingston, Texas, one of 11 children of a poor sharecropper. Raised in abject poverty, he learned to shoot in order to put food on his family's table, and he became an expert marksman because he could not afford to waste ammunition. Lying about his age, he enlisted in the army in June 1942, and although the thin, baby-faced recruit was offered light duty Stateside, he insisted on a combat assignment. Finally detailed to Company B of the 15th Infantry Regiment, he was shipped to North Africa early in 1943, but discovered upon his arrival that the fighting in the area had ended.

Murphy finally got his wish for combat during the invasion of Sicily that July. In the Fifth Army's ensuing Italian campaign his superb marksmanship accounted for more than 150 German fatalities. Thereafter Murphy was promoted to sergeant and in August 1944 assigned to the invasion of southern France.

It was in France that the shy, freckle-faced Texan demonstrated the incredible heroism that made him a living legend. Almost immediately upon his arrival he single-handedly wiped out a German machine-gun squad that had pinned down several American platoons. Promoted to second lieutenant for this display of initiative, he led his company in the Allied advance toward the Rhine, reaching Colmar in eastern France by the end of 1944. When his unit was hit with a massive German counterattack on January 26, 1945, Lieutenant Murphy ordered his men to pull back while he remained at the front to direct mortar fire. When the advancing Nazis reached his position he got atop a disabled tank and, using its machine gun, held them off for over an hour until they fell back. During this encounter he killed or wounded more than 50 of the enemy while receiving a serious injury himself. Murphy's remarkable stand at Colmar won him the Congressional Medal of Honor and capped a list of honors that made him the most decorated U.S. serviceman of the Second World War.

Lieutenant Murphy remained in charge of his unit until the end of the war, advancing as far as Munich before the German surrender. After his return to the United States the 21-year-old hero became a film actor, starring in his autobiography, *To Hell and Back*, the Civil War classic *The Red Badge of Courage*, and a number of Westerns.

Emotionally scarred by his wartime experiences, he was plagued by recurring nightmares and for years could not get to sleep unless he had a loaded pistol under his pillow. He died in an airplane crash on Brush Mountain, Virginia, on May 28, 1971.

(Opposite) Audie Murphy, the boyish-looking hero who became America's most decorated soldier of World War II.

Murphy in "combat," a publicity still from his autobiographical film, *To Hell and Back* (1955).

In August 1917, "Billy" Bishop posed beside his Nieuport 17 in France.
Shortly before this he had become the British Empire's top flier of World
War I.

ALTHOUGH "RED BARON" Manfred von Richthofen and Capt. Eddie Rickenbacker are undoubtedly the best-known pilots of the First World War, many other fliers scored five or more kills during the conflict, thereby becoming aces. One of the most daring of these airmen was the Canadian pilot Billy Bishop, the top flier among the British Commonwealth forces during the war.

William Avery Bishop was born at Owen Sound, Ontario, on February 8, 1894. He received his military training at the Royal Military College at Kingston, and upon his graduation in 1914 he was commissioned a lieutenant of cavalry.

At the onset of the Great War Lieutenant Bishop was ordered to Britain with the Seventh Canadian Mounted Rifles. Realizing, as did Manfred von Richthofen, that cavalrymen would play little or no role in the fighting in Europe, Bishop—like the "Red Baron"—arranged a transfer to the flying corps. The Canadian took to flying immediately, and after a few months he progressed from observer to pilot trainee, winning his wings early in 1916.

After several months of guarding observation blimps in England, Lieutenant Bishop was finally assigned in March 1917 to a combat unit in France—Royal Flying Corps (later RAF) Flight Squadron 60. Bishop performed remarkably well in his new assignment, scoring his initial kill during his first flight on March 25. By the end of April he had chalked up 20 victories and received a promotion to captain.

Captain Bishop became internationally famous for executing the most audacious air raid of the war when he staged a solo attack on a German airfield early on the morning of June 2, downing three planes in the air and seriously damaging several others on the ground. His bravery won him Britain's highest military decoration, the Victoria Cross, and a promotion to major.

The new national hero, Billy Bishop, was sent back to Canada on a recruiting drive in August 1917, but he returned to France in March 1918 to command a squadron of his own. Within three months his score had risen to 72 kills, the highest number of confirmed victories in the RAF (British Maj. Edward Mannock claimed 73, but not all

On August 5 Bishop was promoted to lieutenant colonel and reassigned to staff duties in Britain, putting an end to his brilliant combat career. On his return to Canada he helped organize the Royal Canadian Air Force and then became a successful business executive. During the Second World War he returned to active duty as director of recruiting for the RCAF with the rank of air marshal. William Bishop died at his retirement home in West Palm Beach, Florida, on September 11, 1956, and was buried with full military honors in Toronto, Canada.

Bishop during World War II, while serving as an Air Marshal in the Royal Canadian Air Force. The World War I hero inspired hundreds of young Canadians to enlist as airmen.

THEODORE ROOSEVELT, JR.

United States, 1887–1944

THEODORE ROOSEVELT, JR. was widely regarded as one of the most intrepid fighting generals of the Second World War. In a conflict where top commanders mainly utilized radio communications to direct assaults from the rear, he distinguished himself by his fearless frontline leadership. Indeed he was the only general officer to take part in the first wave of landings during the Normandy invasion.

Roosevelt was born in Oyster Bay, New York, on September 13, 1887. The son of future President Theodore Roosevelt, he was imbued as a child with his father's patriotism and love of "the strenuous life." After graduating from Harvard in 1908, TR, Jr. became a successful businessman in California and New York. He joined the army reserve in 1915 when American involvement in the Great War seemed imminent. After the United States entered the struggle two

years later he was commissioned a captain in the 26th Regiment and sent to France with the First Infantry Division. He gained his reputation as a fighter after being wounded in two battles, winning the Distinguished Service Medal, the Croix de Guerre, and promotion to lieutenant colonel.

Upon his return to the United States Colonel Roosevelt attempted to follow in his father's footsteps and entered politics. He served as a state legislator and assistant secretary of the navy but was defeated in a 1924 bid for governor of New York, ending his hopes for high elected office. He was later appointed governor of Puerto Rico and governor general of the Philippines under President Herbert Hoover.

In April 1941, when war again threatened the United States, Colonel Roosevelt returned to active duty as head of his old unit, the 26th Infantry. Although he was 54 years old he sought a combat command after war

was declared, and FDR, his distant cousin, accomodated him by promoting him to brigadier general in the First Division. Roosevelt first demonstrated his front-line approach to command when he led the initial assault during his unit's baptism of fire at Oran, Algeria, on November 8, 1942. He continued to distinguish himself the following year as second-in-command of the division in Tunisia and Sicily and as the American commander in Sardinia.

In February 1944 General Roosevelt was transferred to Britain as part of the Normandy invasion task force. Assigned as head of the U.S. Fourth Division, he personally led his men on their assault of Utah Beach during the morning of June 6. Throughout the day he calmly walked the beachhead, deploying the newly landed troops and rallying them by his cool display of courage under fire. In the weeks that followed Roosevelt was constantly with his men on the front lines. Exhausted by his efforts, he died of a heart attack at his headquarters near Cherbourg on July 12, 1944. Theodore Roosevelt, Jr. was posthumously awarded the Congressional Medal of Honor for his heroism during the Normandy landing.

(Opposite) Gen. Theodore Roosevelt, Jr., one of World War II's top "fighting generals." "Where the fighting was heaviest, where the progress was slowest, he was there to lead and inspire, and he did it magnificently," one of his men recalled after his death.

Roosevelt in Italy in 1944. The name on his Jeep recalls the Spanish-American War fighting force commanded by his father prior to his becoming president of the United States.

CAPTAIN
EDWARD RICKENBACKER
United States, 1890–1973

THE PILOTS OF the fledgling U.S. Army Air Service were undoubtedly the most colorful figures in the American Expeditionary Force during the First World War. The most famous of these was a former race car driver whose exploits made him a legend in his own time—Capt. Eddie Rickenbacker.

Edward Rickenbacker was born on October 8, 1890, in Columbus, Ohio. The son of Swiss immigrants named Reichenbacher, he changed his surname in response to the anti-German bias in the United States at the beginning of the First World War, adding the middle name Vernon "for class."

Rickenbacker's father died when Eddie was 12, forcing the future air ace to drop out of school and get a job. He had a natural aptitude for mechanics and soon made a name for himself as an automobile engineer and race car driver, setting a world speed record of 134 miles per hour at Daytona in 1911.

When the United States declared war on Germany in 1917 Rickenbacker immediately volunteered for service as an airman, but with his professional background was appointed chauffeur to Gen. Billy Mitchell instead. Dissatisfied with this not very warlike role, Rickenbacker finally wangled a transfer to the Army Air Service as an engineering lieutenant in August 1917. He lost no time beginning flying lessons, and although officially overage, he proved such a good pilot that he won his wings by winter. Assigned to the newly organized 94th Aero Squadron, Lieutenant Rickenbacker scored his first hit on an enemy plane on April 29, 1918. In the month that followed he downed four more, qualifying as one of America's first aces.

Rickenbacker was sidelined for most of summer 1918 with a serious ear infection, but he returned to action with a vengeance on September 24 as captain of his squadron. On the day after he assumed command he won the Con-

gressional Medal of Honor for shooting down two German planes in one raid. By the end of the war six weeks later his score had risen to 26 kills, making him America's top fighter pilot, "the ace of aces."

In the years after the war Captain Eddie, as he preferred to be called, marketed his own car—the Rickenbacker sports sedan—and managed the Indianapolis Speedway. In 1935 he became chief executive of Eastern Airlines, a position that he held until his retirement in 1963. In the Second World War he volunteered as a civilian consultant for the Army Air Force. Shot down over the Pacific during an inspection tour in 1942, he survived for 22 days on a liferaft before being rescued. The amazing Edward Vernon Rickenbacker died during a vacation in Zurich, Switzerland, on July 26, 1973, and is buried in his home town of Columbus, Ohio.

(Opposite) An oil portrait of Capt. "Eddie" Rickenbacker, the United States dashing ace of aces during World War I.

(Right) Captain Eddie behind the guns of one of his first fighters. His unusual habit of aiming with his left eye saved his life during a dogfight in which a German bullet missed him by only an inch on that side.

SIR CLAUDE MacDONALD

United Kingdom, 1852–1915

FOR 55 DAYS in the summer of 1900 the attention of the world was focused on the city of Peking, China. There, the diplomatic legations of 11 nations—the United Kingdom, Germany, Austria, France, Italy, Belgium, Spain, the Netherlands, Russia, Japan, and the United States—were besieged by thousands of fanatical Chinese nationalists called Boxers. The man responsible for coordinating the beleaguered foreigners' defense during this rebellion was Sir Claude MacDonald, the British Minister to the Imperial Manchu court.

MacDonald was born in Scotland on June 12, 1852, the son of Maj. Gen. James MacDonald. Following in his father's footsteps, the younger MacDonald attended the British Royal Military College at Sandhurst in 1868 and was commissioned an officer in Her Majesty's 74th Highlanders in 1872. In recognition of his service during the Egyptian uprising a decade later, he was promoted to major and appointed British military attache in Cairo, thus marking the start of his distinguished career in the British diplomatic corps. After serving in posts throughout Africa for 14 years MacDonald resigned his commission in 1896 to accept an appointment as British minister to Peking. A skillful negotiator, he secured valuable trade concessions in China for the United Kingdom, earning himself a knighthood for his efforts in 1898.

Sir Claude was one of the senior diplomats in Peking when the Boxer Rebellion broke out on June 20, 1900. Angered at the trade agreements that he and other ambassadors had forced from the Manchus, a frenzied throng of Boxers (a secret martial arts society) besieged the walled legation district of Peking to drive the foreign powers from their homeland. The Chinese government refused to intervene, and the 2,000 foreigners in the capital were left to fend for themselves.

As head of the largest legation and the minister with the most military experience, Sir Claude was chosen comman-

der in chief of the international force of 514 soldiers, sailors, and volunteers guarding the 3-acre diplomatic compound. He carefully supervised the fortification of the district, even to the extent of having the ministers' wives sew sandbags and organizing a bucket brigade to extinguish the fires constantly set by the Chinese. MacDonald's defenses were so good that despite limited ammunition his forces were able to withstand repeated attacks by the Box-

ers for 55 days until the legations were rescued by an international relief force on August 14, 1900.

In recognition of his distinguished service in Peking, Sir Claude MacDonald was named a Knight Commander of the Bath and awarded the rank of colonel. Subsequently named British ambassador to Japan, he retired from the foreign service in 1912 and died in London on September 10, 1915.

Sir Claude MacDonald, the resourceful Allied commander in Peking during the Boxer Rebellion. His gentlemanly demeanor belied extensive experience as a British Army officer.

DAVID MARCUS

United States/Israel, 1902–1948

IN THE WAKE OF the Nazi Holocaust Jews from around the world struggled to establish a state of their own in their historic homeland, Palestine. Assisting them in this task was David Marcus, a Jewish officer in the U.S. Army, who as Mickey Stone and later as Mickey Marcus, became the first aluf, or general, of an Israeli military force in 2,000 years.

David Daniel Marcus was born in New York City on February 23, 1902, the son of Jewish immigrants. He entered the U.S. Military Academy in 1920, distinguishing himself as both an athlete and a student. Commissioned a lieutenant of infantry in 1924, he was posted to New York, where he attended law school at night. After receiving his degree in 1927 he resigned from the army to become an attorney.

In 1940, when American entry into the Second World War seemed imminent, Marcus reenlisted in the army as a lieutenant colonel in the Judge Advocate's Corps. After war was declared he was transferred to a combat command with the 17th Division in Hawaii, and in November 1942 was appointed commander of the island's elite Ranger Training School. The following year he was promoted to colonel and named chief of planning for the Civil Affairs Division of Army Intelligence, the unit responsible for the administration of captured enemy territories. Transferred to the European theater he participated in the invasion of Normandy with the 101st Airborne Division and later served as Gen. George C. Patton's liaison with liberated concentration camp prisoners. He finished the war as chief of the army's war crimes branch, preparing cases for the Nuremberg trials.

In 1947 Marcus resigned from the army and returned to his family in New York. Shortly thereafter, he was asked to serve as a military adviser to the Israeli force being formed in Palestine in preparation for the creation of a Jewish homeland. Although he was loath to leave his home again so soon, he accepted the job. Assuming the name Mickey Stone, he coordinated the organization and training of the provisional Israeli army and played a key role in developing a battle plan for the war with the neighboring Arab states that broke out after Israel's declaration of statehood on May 14, 1948.

When the Israeli's campaign for the key city of Jerusalem faltered later that month, Marcus was put in charge of the offensive. He quickly reversed the Israeli's losses, opening a roadway between Tel Aviv and the beleaguered Holy City and securing its western section as part of the State of Israel. Three days later, on the morning of June 11, 1948, he was tragically killed outside of his headquarters near Jerusalem by a sentry. He was subsequently given a hero's burial at the U.S. Military Academy and posthumously awarded Israel's Order of Independence.

David "Mickey" Marcus, the American career soldier who became the first commanding general of the Israeli Army. He is pictured at his headquarters on June 9, 1948, following his greatest triumph, the capture of western Jerusalem.

LIEUTENANT GENERAL
CLAIRE CHENNAULT
United States, 1893–1958

BEFORE THE UNITED STATES entered the Second World War, many Americans concerned with the rise of the Axis powers enlisted in foreign armed forces. The most famous of these American volunteers were China's legendary Flying Tigers, led by the indomitable Gen. Claire Chennault.

Claire Lee Chennault was born in Commerce, Texas, on September 6, 1893. Raised in Louisiana, he received his initial military training while a student at the state university. When the United States entered the First World War he volunteered for the Army's Air Service but was assigned to the infantry. Undaunted, he took flying lessons on his own and was finally commissioned a lieutenant in the Air Service in 1920.

Over the next decade Chennault became one of the army's top fliers and the country's leading expert on aerial fighter tactics, authoring a definitive study, *The Role of Defensive Pursuit*, in 1935. His theories received widespread attention overseas but were downplayed by the bomber-oriented American high command, and he was edged into retirement with the rank of captain at the beginning of 1937.

After leaving the army, Chennault was hired to head a small group of instructors who would train the Chinese air force. When the Sino-Japanese War erupted in July 1937 he became Generalissimo Chiang Kai-shek's top air commander, leading the heavily outnumbered Chinese fighter pilots in a series of stunning victories against the Japanese bombers. By early 1941 Chennault's actions, which had initially been disowned by the American government, were seen as so important to the balance of power in the Far East that he was given permission to pur-

Claire Lee Chennault, organizer of the legendary Flying Tigers and one of the world's top experts on air tactics. On his shoulder is the distinctive patch of the U.S. Far Eastern Command; the Flying Tigers had previously used a winged tiger insignia.

General Chennault inspecting one of the P-51s which formed the backbone of the Allied air force in China late in the war. By early 1945, his planes had driven the Japanese from the Chinese skies.

Chennault (left) directing operations from a mobile command post during a Japanese air raid early in 1944. A tough fighter who enjoyed being in the thick of the action, he is—typically—the only man in the photo not wearing a helmet.

chase 100 American planes and to recruit pilots in the United States. The American Volunteer Group that emerged—commonly known as the "Flying Tigers" after the tiger shark jaws painted on their P-40s—grew into one of the finest air forces in the world, downing some 450 Japanese Zeros in China and Burma between October 1941 and July 1942 with losses of only 26 of its own men.

After America's entry into the war, the Flying Tigers were incorporated into the U.S. Army, and Chennault, appointed a major general, led the unit to even

greater successes. Indeed, by March 1945 they had virtually annihilated the Japanese air force in China. The general was awarded China's highest military decoration, the Order of the Blue Sky and White Sun, becoming the first foreigner ever to be so honored. But shortly thereafter he was removed from his command, the result of his long-standing feud with Gen. "Vinegar Joe" Stilwell. Deeply insulted, he resigned from the army to establish an air transport line in the Far East.

On July 18, 1958, a grateful nation finally acknowledged Claire Chennault's immense wartime contributions by promoting him to lieutenant general, retired. Nine days later he died of cancer in New Orleans, Louisiana.

HENRY JOHNSON

United States, ca. 1897–1929

OF THE 4.5 MILLION doughboys who served in the U.S. Army during the First World War, 400,000 were African-Americans. The most famous of these soldiers was Henry Johnson, the first American private to receive the Croix de Guerre during the war and one of the toughest fighting men in the American Expeditionary Force.

Henry Johnson was born in Winston-Salem, North Carolina, around 1897. A few years later his family moved to Albany, New York, where Henry was raised. Although small, the lad developed a reputation as a tough fighter, learning on the streets the combat skills he would later employ so effectively in France.

When the United States declared war on Germany on April 6, 1917, Johnson was working as a porter in the Albany railroad station. Dissatisfied with his life and wishing to serve his country, he enlisted on June 5 as a private in New York's all-African-American 15th National Guard. The regiment was quickly accepted into Federal service and after a brief training period embarked for France that November.

Shortly after arriving in Europe, Private Johnson's unit was assigned to the French army, which had a more open-minded attitude toward nonwhite troops than did the Americans. Redesignated the 369th Infantry Regiment (U.S.), the battalion arrived at the front on March 20, 1917, thus becoming the first American forces to face combat in the war.

It was during the unit's first brush with the enemy, on the night of May 13, that Pvt. Henry Johnson earned his place among the heroes of the War to End All Wars. While on guard duty in the trenches at Montplaisir Johnson and his partner, Pvt. Needham Roberts, were attacked by a German raiding party of two dozen soldiers. Although severely wounded Johnson managed to kill four of the Germans, stabbing two of them with his knife as they attempted to carry off Private Roberts. He then single-handedly drove off the remainder of the party with grenades, stopping only when he fainted from a loss of blood. In recognition of what the American newspapers quickly dubbed "the Battle of Henry Johnson," the brave private was awarded the Croix de Guerre with Palm and cited by Generals John J. Pershing and Ferdinand Foch for "magnificent courage and energy." Upon his release from the hospital he was promoted to sergeant and given light duties for the duration of the war, being too badly injured to return to the front.

When the 369th Regiment returned to New York in February 1919 Sergeant Johnson was greeted as a hero. The fame soon passed, however, and since he was too seriously disabled to get a steady job, his life was not easy. Henry Johnson died as a result of his wounds at Walter Reed Army Hospital in Washington, D.C., on July 2, 1929, and is buried in Arlington National Cemetery.

Henry Johnson, the most famous African-American soldier of World War I.

RICHARD BONG
United States, 1920–1945

THE ONSET OF THE Second World War brought the thrill of the dogfight to a new generation of combat pilots flying a new breed of plane, faster and vastly more maneuverable than those of the First World War. Among the best of these pilots was the young major destined to become America's all-time top ace, Richard Bong.

Richard Ira Bong was born in Superior, Wisconsin, on September 24, 1920, the son of Swedish immigrant Carl Bong and his wife Dora Bryce. Raised on the family farm near Poplar, Wisconsin, Richard was attending Superior Teachers College when the United States entered the Second World War. Dropping out of school, he enlisted in the Army Air Corps on May 19, 1941, and signed up for flight training, earning his wings the following January. Commissioned a lieutenant, he spent several months stateside as an instructor before being sent to New Guinea in September.

Assigned to the Fifth Air Force, Bong was detailed as flight leader of the "Flying Knight" squadron in November. Within a year he had made five confirmed kills, becoming an ace. He was then sent back to the United States for advanced gunnery training, which he found invaluable. Early in 1944, within four months of his return to the Pacific, he became one of the first American

fliers to break Capt. Eddie Rickenbacker's First World War record of 28 kills. In one spectacular engagement alone, Bong downed three Japanese Zeros and outran another six.

Although he was promoted to major and detailed as a base gunnery instructor in May, Bong continued to volunteer for combat over New Guinea, Borneo, and Leyte. He was awarded the Congressional Medal of Honor that summer, topping off an impressive list of decorations that included the Distinguished Service Cross, two Silver Stars, seven Distinguished Flying Crosses, and 15 Air Medals.

On December 17 Major Bong made his 40th kill, establishing him as America's ace of aces. Following this accomplishment, he was transferred to California as a test pilot. Tragically Bong, the survivor of 500 hours of combat against the Japanese, died when an experimental jet he was piloting exploded over North Hollywood on August 6, 1945.

(Right) Richard Bong in the cockpit of his P-38 fighter after scoring his 27th kill, as noted by painted Japanese flags on the plane's fuselage.

(Below) Major Bong (right) is congratulated on his superb combat record by America's top World War I ace, Capt. Eddie Rickenbacker. In 1944 Bong became the first Army Air Force pilot to break Rickenbacker's record of 26 kills.

PILOT
.B.I.OONG.

—IMPORTANT—
MAXIMUM MANEUVERABILITY
REQUIRES EDGE OF FILLET
TO FIT TIGHTLY ON
WINDOW FILLER STRIP

THE FIRST WORLD WAR created many popular heroes, men like Alvin York, Manfred von Richthofen, "Black Jack" Pershing, and John Jellicoe. Perhaps the most famous of all was a rather unconventional British lieutenant colonel named Thomas Edward Lawrence—the legendary "Lawrence of Arabia."

Lawrence was born in Tremadoc, Wales, on August 15, 1888, the illegitimate son of Sir Thomas Chapman, a wealthy landowner, and Sarah Maden. Ned—as young Lawrence was called—developed an interest in the Near East while studying for his history degree at Oxford University. Following his graduation in 1910 he spent four years in Syria with an archaeological expedition sponsored by the British Museum, during which time he learned to speak several Arabic dialects and became an expert on local customs and traditions. Lawrence was on leave in Britain at the outbreak of the First World War. When Turkey allied itself with Germany in October 1914, bringing the war to the Ottoman Empire's territories in the Near East, the diminutive archaeologist volunteered his services to the Intelligence Section of the British army. Commissioned a second lieutenant, he was immediately detailed to the Arab Bureau at British headquarters in Cairo, Egypt.

In October 1916, after two years in Cairo, Lawrence was finally given the active role he craved when he was assigned to coordinate the Arab's guerrilla warfare against the Turks in western Arabia. Lawrence began by leading his highly mobile forces in a series of raids against the strategic railway that supplied the Turkish base at Medina and then culminated his campaign by capturing the Red Sea port of Aqaba on July 6, 1917. That daring operation earned "Lawrence of Arabia" international fame, a promotion to major, and additional support from his commander, Gen. Edmund Allenby. In the year that followed Lawrence's Arab tribesmen thoroughly disrupted Ottoman operations in the area, isolating the garrison at Medina and driving the Turks northward. Lawrence climaxed his operations with the capture of Damascus, Syria, on October 1, 1918, effectively ending the Allies' struggle against the Turks in the Near East.

Following the capture of Damascus Lawrence, who was promoted to lieutenant colonel, hurried back to Europe. There he protested British and French plans to place the Arabs under their tutelage instead of giving them full independence as had been promised. After the war, he returned to Oxford, where he wrote his epic history of the Arabian campaign, *Seven Pillars of Wisdom*. Tiring of the lack of privacy his fame had brought him, he enlisted in the ranks of the RAF in 1922 under an assumed name. He retired from active duty in February 1935 and died from injuries sustained in a motorcycle accident at Bovington, England, on May 13, 1935.

(Above) T. E. Lawrence after World War I. He loved the thrill of high speed—some say he became addicted to it—and died in a motorcycle accident in 1935.

(Opposite) The enigmatic Lawrence of Arabia in the native costume that made him one of the most colorful and well-known military figures of World War I.

JOHN F. KENNEDY

United States, 1917–1963

THE NATURE OF NAVAL combat, with carefully trained crews fighting as one and ships closely acting in concert, does not usually lend itself to individual heroics the way that air and land combat do. For this reason only one junior naval officer has been selected for inclusion among the "Fighting Men" of this book. Nevertheless, he is among the most famous American heroes of this century—Lt. John Kennedy.

John Fitzgerald Kennedy was born in Brookline, Massachusetts, on May 29, 1917, the second son of prominent Democratic politician and multi-millionaire Joseph Kennedy, Sr. After graduating from Harvard in 1940 Jack attempted to enlist in the army but was rejected due to a back injury suffered while playing football. Through corrective exercise and his father's political

connections he was commissioned an ensign in the Naval Reserve in September 1941 and assigned to naval intelligence at the Pentagon. Following Pearl Harbor Kennedy volunteered for training as commander of a patrol torpedo (PT) boat. Completing the course in January 1943, he was promoted to lieutenant (j.g.) and assigned to the Solomon Islands, at the center of the war in the Pacific.

Upon his arrival at Tulagi on April 12, Lieutenant Kennedy was assigned command of the PT-109, a battle-scarred vessel in port for overhaul. The IO9's patrols were fairly quiet until the early morning of August 2, when she was making a reconnaissance near the island of Kolombangara. Discovered at close quarters in the gloom by the fast-moving Japanese destroyer *Amagiri*, she was rammed and split in half before

(Opposite) The strain of John F. Kennedy's heroic efforts following the sinking of PT-109 shows clearly in this photograph taken shortly after his crew's rescue. Within a few months the lieutenant was forced to accept a medical discharge from the navy.

(Below) In July 1943, Kennedy (right) posed for a photographer with members of his crew on the deck of PT-109. The Japanese destroyer *Amaqiri* rammed the boat just behind the spot where this picture was taken.

Kennedy's war record helped him to win the presidency of the United States in 1960. Tie clasps in the shape of PT-109 became cherished momentos of his administration.

Lieutenant Kennedy could maneuver her out of the way. After the Japanese ship dashed on, Kennedy was able to gather together his ten surviving crewmen and lead them in a 3¹/₂ mile swim to the closest safe island, towing the worst-injured man behind him by holding the belt from his life jacket in his teeth.

After a week of dodging Japanese patrols, Kennedy and his men were discovered by friendly natives. They smuggled Jack to an Allied radio post where he was able to arrange for the rescue of himself and his crew. His bravery won him the Navy and Marine Corps Medal, promotion to full lieutenant, and command of a new torpedo boat, PT-59. Shortly thereafter, however, he was relieved of duty at doctor's orders—the result of his injuries from the sinking of PT-109.

After his recovery Kennedy turned to politics. His intelligence, good looks, and war record combined with his father's influence made him a perfect candidate, and he quickly won election to the House and later the Senate from Massachusetts. In 1960 he became the youngest man ever elected President of the United States. He was assassinated by Lee Harvey Oswald in Dallas, Texas, on November 22, 1963.

GROUP CAPTAIN
SIR DOUGLAS BADER
United Kingdom, 1910–1982

THE IMMENSE CONTRIBUTION of the Royal Air Force during the Battle of Britain was aptly described by Sir Winston Churchill: "Never in the field of human conflict was so much owed by so many to so few." Perhaps the most remarkable of the 2,500 RAF fliers who composed "the few" was the indomitable Douglas Bader, who became one of Britain's finest fighter pilots despite the loss of his legs before the war.

Douglas Robert Stewart Bader was born in London, England, on February 21, 1910, the son of a Royal Army Engineer. A good student and outstanding athlete, Bader was accepted into the Royal Air Force College at Cranwell in 1928, graduating second in his class two years later. Assigned to the No. 23 Squadron at Kenley, he was on his way to becoming one of the RAF's top stunt pilots when his plane crashed during an aerial exhibition on December 14, 1931. Bader escaped with his life, but both his legs had to be amputated. The resilient young officer did not allow the accident to ruin his life, and after being fitted with artificial legs he returned to duty early in 1933. Despite the fact that he could still drive, play tennis, and golf, Bader was considered too crippled to fly and was relegated to a ground assignment. Disgusted, he resigned from the RAF in April and took a job with an aircraft company.

When Britain entered the Second World War in 1939 Douglas Bader again offered his services to the RAF, and this time the veteran pilot was gladly accepted. Appointed a flight commander with Squadron No. 222, he saw his first combat when he provided air cover to British ground forces during the evacuation from Dunkirk in May 1940. During the Battle of Britain he led the 12th Group Wing to a record 152 kills with only 30 losses of its own, earning the Distinguished Service Order and the Distinguished Flying Cross. Promoted to wing commander, he subsequently scored more than two dozen kills against the Luftwaffe in France before being downed himself on August 9, 1941. Captured by the Germans after parachuting to safety, the irrepressible Bader made four escape attempts during the years that followed. He was finally incarcerated in the Nazis' maxi-

The indomitable Sir Douglas Bader touring a British foundry after the war. The legless flier made frequent personal appearances to promote hiring the handicapped.

mum-security prisoner-of-war camp at Colditz, where the guards put an end to his breakouts by confiscating his legs every night.

After Douglas Bader was liberated from Colditz in 1945 he returned to active duty with the RAF and, promoted to group captain, led its victorious flypast over London on September 15. He retired from the service the following year to become head of Shell Oil's aircraft division. An inspiration to those

with physical handicaps, Bader regularly worked with the disabled at hospitals and schools, for which he was knighted in 1976. Sir Douglas Bader died in London on September 5, 1982.

ALVIN YORK

ALVIN YORK IS one of the most remarkable figures in the annals of military history. A backwoods farm boy who almost left the army as a conscientious objector, he instead became the most famous American hero of the First World War with his single-handed capture of an entire German machine-gun battalion of over 100 men.

Alvin Cullum York was born in Pall Mall, Tennessee, on December 13, 1887. Raised in the mountains of rural Tennessee, he learned to shoot as a boy, becoming an expert with both pistol and rifle. Under the influence of his future wife, Gracie Williams, he also became a devout born-again Christian, giving up the drinking, gambling, and fighting that had marked his younger days.

When drafted into the army in 1917, York sought exemption as a conscientious objector but was turned down. Inducted into the 328th Infantry Regiment on November 24, he distinguished himself in basic training until he was ordered to shoot at human forms on the the target range. At first he refused. But, after days of soul-searching, the earnest fundamentalist finally reconciled himself to military service, completed his training, and sailed to France with his unit the following spring.

Alvin York's regiment was assigned to the Meuse-Argonne salient. There on the morning of October 8, 1918, during the American advance against the firmly entrenched German line, his company was ordered to attack a heavily guarded hill near Châtel-Chéhéry. Pinned down by machine-gun fire, York—by then a corporal—joined a squad of 17 men in an attempt to out-flank the German position. After capturing 20 German soldiers the Americans were discovered, and the fire of the entire machine-gun battalion concentrated upon them. Within minutes the squad was cut down to just seven men, with Corporal York the senior remaining NCO.

York worked his way to a point where he had a good line of fire and quickly picked off 17 of the German gunners with his rifle. After he shot eight more with his pistol the Germans had enough, and the entire battalion of 112 surrendered to the corporal, making a total of 132 prisoners that he and his squad brought back to headquarters.

Alvin York was subsequently promoted to sergeant and awarded the Congressional Medal of Honor for his amazing feat. At the close of the war he returned to Tennessee, married Gracie Williams, and settled on a farm presented to him by his grateful home state. The modest hero turned down many offers for endorsements, claiming, "This uniform ain't for sale," and used the proceeds from the book and movie of his life story to establish schools for poor mountain children. Sergeant York died in Nashville, Tennessee, on September 2, 1964.

(Opposite) Sgt. Alvin York, America's leading hero of World War I, wearing his Congressional Medal of Honor and Croix de Guerre.

(Left) York returned to his home state of Tennessee after the war and spent the remainder of his life trying to improve living conditions in the mountain country were he was raised.

GREGORY BOYINGTON

United States, 1912–1988

AIR COMBAT WAS MORE decisive in the island-hopping Pacific theater of the Second World War than in any other area of operations. Among the best of the Allied fliers in the struggle against the Japanese was the commander of the Black Sheep Squadron, top Marine Corps ace Gregory "Pappy" Boyington.

Gregory Boyington was born in Coeur d'Alene, Idaho, on December 4, 1912, and raised on his father's farms in Idaho and nearby Washington. Enlisting in the U.S. Marine Corps Reserve as an aviation cadet in 1936, he proved to be an excellent pilot, winning his wings and a lieutenant's commission the following year.

In August 1941, while an instructor at the Marine Corps flying school at Pensacola, Florida, Boyington was recruited as one of Gen. Claire Chennault's Flying Tigers. Resigning from the marines with the promise of reinstatement at the end of his service with Chennault, Boyington left for the Tigers' base in Toungoo, Burma, that November. He downed his first Japanese Zero during his initial combat flight in January, and by the end of June had scored five more hits, qualifying as an ace.

When the Tigers were attatched to the U.S. Army Air Force in July 1942 Boyington, like any self-respecting leatherneck, refused to go along. He returned to the United States, invoked his reen-

listment clause, and in November was commissioned a major in the marines. Detailed to the air base at Espiritu Santo in the Solomon Islands, he organized a new fighter squadron composed of unassigned pilots, who dubbed themselves "Boyington's Bastards" (the name was later cleaned up to the Black Sheep Squadron). Major Boyington, at age 30, was called "Pappy" by his 19-year-old trainees, but they followed the "old man" through a series of highly successful raids which led to the downing of almost 200 Japanese planes. During these sorties Boyington increased his total to 28 kills, becoming the first American pilot to break Capt. Eddie Rickenbacker's First World War combat record and the marines' top ace of the war.

Boyington downed his last plane on January 3, 1944. Moments later he was shot down himself over the Coral Sea. Captured by a Japanese submarine, he was held in Ofuna Prisoner-of-War Camp near Yokohama, Japan, until August 1945. On his return to the United States he was promoted to lieutenant colonel and awarded the Congressional Medal of Honor for his outstanding combat record. He resigned from the marines later that year and subsequently authored a best-selling memoir of his wartime experiences entitled *Baa Baa Black Sheep.* Boyington died in Fresno, California, on January 11, 1988.

(Right) Gregory "Pappy" Boyington, tough, resolute and every inch a Marine flier.

(Far right) Major Boyington (front row, third from right) and his Black Sheep Squadron pictured on one of the Corsair fighters that they used on their missions.

CHARLES WHITTLESEY

United States, 1884–1921

THE UNITED STATES HAS had few less likely heroes than Charles Whittlesey. A bookish New York attorney who hated war, Colonel Whittlesey displayed unwavering dedication to duty as commander of the famed "Lost Battalion," making him one of the leading fighting men of the Great War.

Charles Whittlesey was born in Florence, Wisconsin, on January 20, 1884. A descendant of some of New England's oldest families, he was raised in Pittsfield, Massachusetts, and educated at Williams and at Harvard, where he received his law degree in 1908. The young attorney began his practice in New York, and by 1911 was successful enough to open his own law office.

When the United States entered the First World War in 1917 Whittlesey's high sense of social duty and *noblesse oblige* led him to volunteer as an officer in the army. Commissioned a captain in the 308th Infantry Regiment, the former Wall Street lawyer arrived in France in April 1918. Promoted to major he received his baptism of fire during the fighting on the Aisne River that September.

Major Whittlesey was catapulted to fame during the American Expeditionary Force's Argonne offensive in October. While leading two battalions totaling 800 men in an assault against the German line near Charlevaux, Whittlesey became cut off from his slower-moving support units. Under strict orders not to retreat, he established a defensive position in the woods and waited for reinforcements to catch up; they never arrived, and Whittlesey's men found themselves surrounded by German infantry. For five days the soldiers of the "Lost Battalion"—as it became known—held their ground against repeated German assaults despite casualties which cut their fighting strength to fewer than 200 men. Through attacks by artillery, machine guns, and flamethrowers Whittlesey's men held firm, and when the German commander finally demanded his surrender on the morning of October 7 he refused to even reply.

The survivors of the "Lost Battalion" were rescued by an American advance on the evening of October 7. When Major Whittlesey's determined stand was made known he was hailed by General Pershing as one of the AEF's greatest heroes, awarded the Congressional Medal of Honor, and promoted to lieutenant colonel.

After the Armistice Colonel Whittlesey returned to New York to resume his law practice, but he had difficulty forgetting the horrors of war and adjusting to his new-found fame. Shortly after serving as one of the honorary pallbearers at the dedication of the Tomb of the Unknown Soldier in Washington, D.C., Whittlesey committed suicide by jumping from the steamer *Toloa* en route to Havana, Cuba, on the evening of November 25, 1921.

The scholarly Col. Charles Whittlesey, commander of the famed Lost Battalion of World War I.

THE VIETNAM WAR was the most divisive conflict in recent American history. One of the few popular heroes to emerge from this unpopular struggle was "Bull" Simons, the tough-as-nails Green Beret colonel who led a daring mission to rescue American prisoners of war in the heart of North Vietnam.

Arthur D. Simons was born in New York City on June 28, 1918. He joined the Reserve Officer Training Corps while a journalism student at the University of Missouri, and upon his graduation a few months after America's entry into the Second World War was commissioned a lieutenant in the army. Assigned to the Pacific theater, he received his initial commando training with the Rangers in New Guinea and the Philippines. After the war he attended the army's Special Warfare School, and in the early 1960s became one of the first officers in the Green Berets, serving in Panama, Laos, and Vietnam.

In July 1970, Simons, by then a colonel and one of America's most experienced special operations officers, was selected to lead a mission designed to free the American servicemen held in the Son Tay Prisoner-of-War Camp located 23 miles west of Hanoi. He carefully trained his troops in every aspect of the operation at a replica of the camp in Florida, and on November 20 led them into action at Son Tay. Although no prisoners were rescued—they had all been moved before the raid—the mission was a major boost to American morale and Simons was awarded the Distinguished Service Cross in a special White House ceremony. Two years later, after retiring from the army, he was the guest of honor at a San Francisco parade for returning POWs sponsored by Texas businessman H. Ross Perot.

When two of Perot's executives in Tehran were arrested at the beginning of the Iranian revolution in December 1978, he turned to Simons for help. Within two months the former Green Beret had organized and executed a rescue mission, freeing the Americans in a daring jailbreak. Returning with them to Texas, Simons remained a guest at Perot's Dallas estate until his death on May 21, 1979.

Arthur Simons, the soldier's soldier who led daring rescue operations in both Vietnam and Iran. On meeting him, a respectful John Wayne declared, "You *are* the hero I only play in the movies."

LUCIAN TRUSCOTT
United States, 1895–1965

THE ARMED FORCES OF the United States include some of the finest elite combat units in the world, including the Army Green Berets, the Delta Force, and the Navy Seals. All of them trace their roots to the nation's oldest commando unit, the U.S. Army Rangers, founded by one of the Second World War's toughest fighting men, Gen. Lucian Truscott.

Lucian King Truscott, Jr. was born in Chatfield, Texas, on January 9, 1895. Raised in Oklahoma, he received a degree in education from the state college in 1911 and taught at local schools until his enlistment in the army at the outbreak of the Great War. After attending officer's training camp he was commissioned a lieutenant in the 17th Cavalry and stationed in Arizona.

At the end of the war Truscott remained in the cavalry, rising to the rank of major in 1936 and serving as an instructor in the Army Command and Staff School at Fort Leavenworth, Kansas. He was subsequently transferred to an armored command at Fort Knox, Kentucky, and then detailed to staff work in Washington, D.C., where he was promoted to colonel.

Shortly after the United States entered the Second World War Truscott was upgraded to brigadier general and given the task of forming an elite unit modeled after Britain's Commandos. He called them the Rangers, after Rogers' Rangers, a crack American fighting outfit in the French and Indian War. He put his recruits—top fighting men from throughout the service—through a grueling course of specialized training which made them the toughest troops in the army. General Truscott gained their respect by doing everything he expected them to do. In just two months he had them ready for their first mission, an Allied raid on Dieppe, France. In November 1942, during the North African campaign, they captured Port Lyautey, Morocco, earning their commander a well-deserved promotion to major general and the Distinguished Service Medal.

With the Rangers fully established, General Truscott was transferred to Tunisia in December as commander of Patton's Third Division. Thereafter he spearheaded the assaults on Palermo, Sicily, and on Salerno and Anzio on the Italian mainland. Inspiring his men with

Gen. Lucian Truscott, the tough-as-nails founder of the U.S. Army Rangers.

his constant presence at the front, he continued to score impressive victories during the invasion of southern France in 1944. Winning promotion to lieutenant general, he finished the war as head of the Fifth Army in Italy, succeeding Gen. Mark Clark in December 1944.

At the war's conclusion General Truscott replaced George Patton as military governor of Bavaria. He retired from the army in 1947, and in 1954 was retroactively promoted to full general. He died in Washington, D.C., on September 12, 1965.

WILLIAM DONOVAN

United States, 1883–1959

WILLIAM DONOVAN HAD one of the most remarkable and influential military careers in modern American history. A winner of the Congressional Medal of Honor during the Great War, "Wild Bill" Donovan became America's premier spymaster during the Second World War, playing such a pivotal role in the Allied victory that Dwight D. Eisenhower dubbed him America's "Last Hero."

William Joseph Donovan was born in Buffalo, New York, on January 1, 1883. An excellent student, he received a law degree from Columbia University in 1907, just two years after receiving a B.A. from that institution. Returning to

Buffalo, he became a successful attorney and helped organize a National Guard cavalry troop. Elected captain, Donovan got his first command experience in 1916 when the unit was called up for duty in Texas during Gen. John J. Pershing's Mexican border campaign. The young neophyte's no-nonsense, professional attitude earned him the respect of his fellow officers and the nickname "Wild Bill" from his men.

Donovan's performance in Texas so impressed the commanders of New York's famed 69th Regiment—the "Fighting Irish"—that he was recruited as the unit's major when the United States entered the First World War. Sent to France with the American Expedi-

tionary Force's Rainbow Division, "Wild Bill" won the Distinguished Service Cross and promotion to lieutenant colonel in August 1918 for his bravery under fire at the Battle of the Marne. Two months later, during the Argonne offensive, he earned the Congressional Medal of Honor for leading the regiment in an extended assault without regard to his own life-threatening injuries.

After returning to the United States as a full colonel in 1919 Donovan resumed his law practice and entered politics, winning appointment as Assistant U.S. Attorney General in 1925. During his years in Washington, D.C., he became known as an astute analyst of international military affairs. In 1929, he returned to private practice but made several trips thereafter to Europe and Africa as an "unofficial" government observer. With the outbreak of the Second World War in 1939 his missions became increasingly more important; Donovan's assessment of Britain's ability to carry on the war, for example, convinced President Franklin D. Roosevelt to offer that country American military assistance in 1940. When the United States entered the war the following year, "Wild Bill" was the logical choice to organize the nation's wartime intelligence network, the Office of Strategic Services. Promoted to major general, he supervised espionage activities in every theater of the war except the Pacific, where Gen. Douglas MacArthur insisted on running his own intelligence operation. Tough as ever, the 60-year-old Donovan refused to be tied to an office and personally visited every front from China to Morocco, even taking part in the landings at Sicily, Anzio, and Normandy.

At the close of the war, when the OSS was disbanded, General Donovan helped prepare cases against high-ranking Nazis during the Nuremberg war crimes trials. He later served as ambassador to Thailand. In 1957, he received the National Security Medal, the country's highest intelligence decoration. He died in Washington, D.C., on February 8, 1959.

"Wild Bill" Donovan as head of the Office of Strategic Services during World War II. His hard work and insight laid the groundwork for the creation of the Central Intelligence Agency after the war.

CAPTAIN
MANFRED VON RICHTHOFEN
Germany, 1892–1918

THE FIRST WORLD WAR saw the development of several new forms of weaponry including poison gas and mechanized tanks, but none was as important to 20th-century military science as the airplane. One of the men who did the most to demonstrate the importance of air power in combat was the conflict's most famous flier, Germany's "Red Baron," Manfred von Richthofen.

Von Richthofen was born in Schweidnitz, Germany, on May 2, 1892. A member of the Prussian nobility, young Manfred was educated at the military school at Wahlstatt and the Royal Military Academy at Gross Lichterfelde. Upon his graduation in 1911 he was assigned to a mounted regiment, the First Uhlans, and commissioned a lieutenant the following year.

At the beginning of the Great War von Richthofen's unit was assigned to the western front. Trench warfare and machine guns soon eliminated horse cavalry from the fighting, and von Richthofen, eager for combat, sought transfer to a more active branch of service. Toward the end of 1914 he succeeded in obtaining an appointment to the Army Air Service as an observer. At that point in the war aircraft were primarily used for reconnaissance, but when pilots started engaging in aerial combat von Richthofen eagerly signed up for flying lessons, qualifying as a pilot on December 25, 1915.

Fighting on both the eastern and western fronts, the 23-year-old lieutenant quickly began making a name for himself. By December 1916 he was credited with 12 kills, including that of the leading British ace, Maj. Lanoe Hawker, for which von Richthofen received Prussia's highest military decoration, the Pour le Mérite—a blue cross commonly known as the Blue Max.

As one of Germany's top aces von Richthofen was awarded his own command, Jagdstaffel ("hunting group") 11, on January 16, 1917. Dubbed the "Flying Circus" because of its brightly painted aircraft—von Richthofen himself flew a scarlet Albatros DII, which earned him the nickname "the Red Baron"—the unit soon became Germany's leading fighter group. Throughout that winter von Richthofen continued to add to his already impressive list of kills, and by the time he was promoted to captain in April he had become a living legend to the Allies as well as the Germans.

On April 20, 1918, Baron von Richthofen downed his 80th plane, becoming the top ace on either side during the war. The following day he was shot down near Amiens and killed, either by Canadian airman Roy Brown or by ground fire from Sir John Monash's Australians. Respectful Allied pilots laid the "Red Baron" to rest in Bertangles, France, beneath a wreath inscribed "To our gallant and worthy foe." In 1925 von Richthofen's remains were moved to Berlin, where he was interred as a national hero.

(Below) The legendary Red Baron, Manfred von Richthofen. Below his collar he is wearing Imperial Germany's highest military decoration, the coveted "Blue Max."

(Right) A Fokker Dr. I Triplane of the type Von Richthofen's "Flying Circus" used. The inscription identifies it as "the model plane in which Manfred von Richthofen met a hero's death in aerial combat on April 21, 1918."

FIGHTING MEN

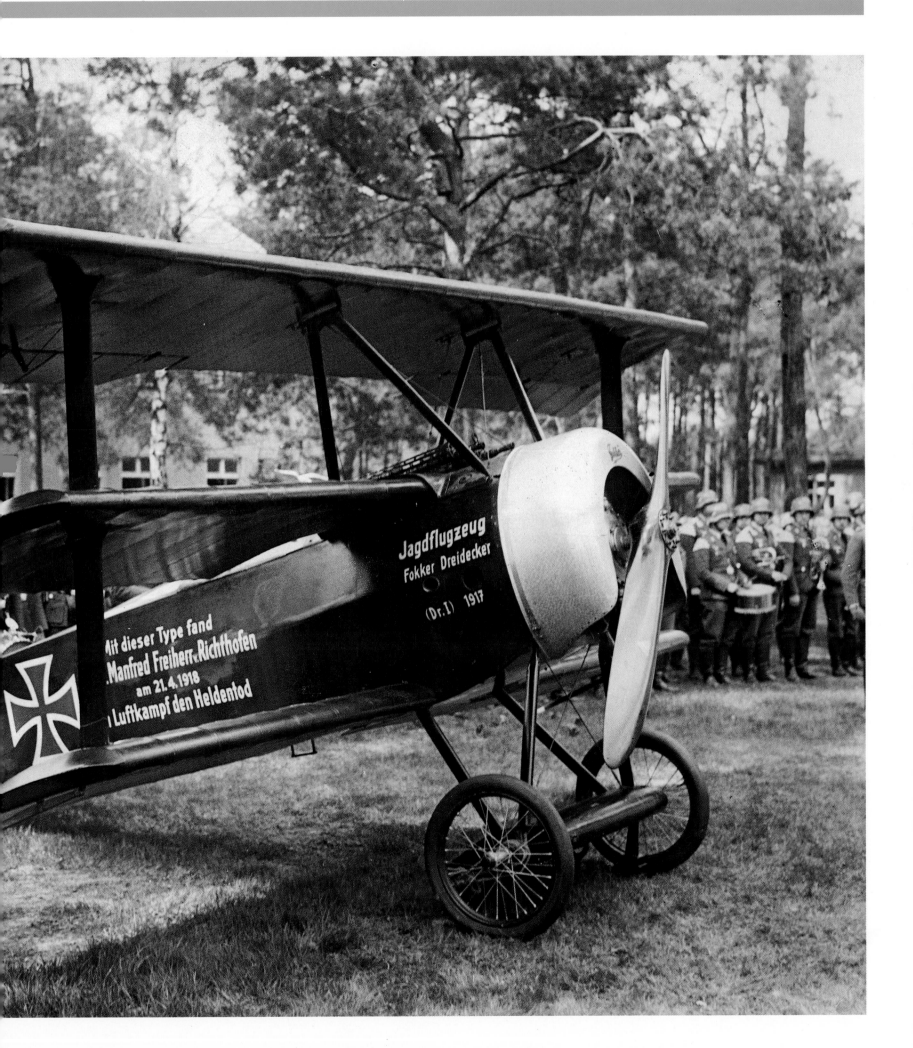

Jagdflugzeug
Fokker Dreidecker
(Dr.I) 1917

Mit dieser Type fand
Manfred Freiherr v. Richthofen
am 21.4.1918
n Luftkampf den Heldentod

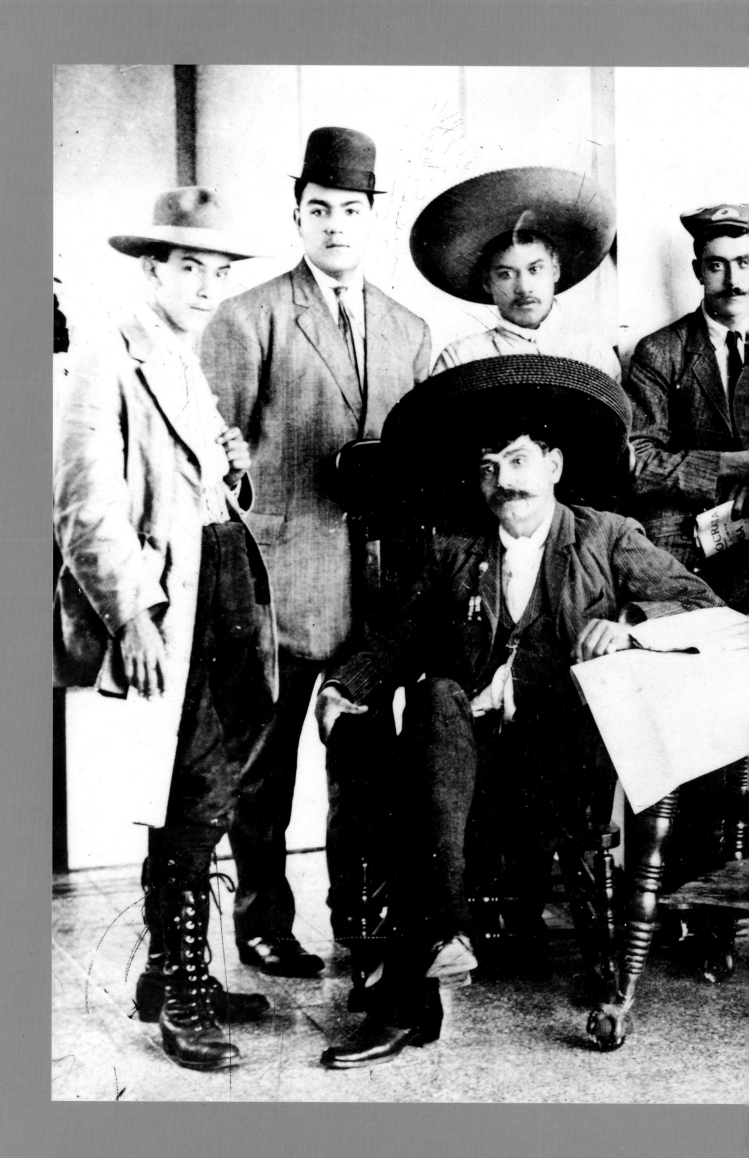

The Mexican revolutionary, Emiliano Zapata (seated center), and his principal lieutenants.

REBELS

CHAIRMAN
MAO ZEDONG
China, 1893–1976

MAO ZEDONG WAS, with Sun Yat-sen and Chiang Kai-shek, one of the three most important figures in modern Chinese history. A brilliant military and political leader, Mao engineered the Red Army's victory over Chiang's Nationalists in a Communist triumph whose magnitude was comparable only to that of the Russian Revolution.

Mao Zedong was born to a peasant family in Shaoshan, China, on December 26, 1893. Raised in the poverty of rural Hunan province, he developed a hatred of the Imperial Chinese government while a boy, and in 1911 left school to join the revolution against Manchu rule. In the years that followed Mao grew increasingly more radical, and in 1921 became one of the founding members of the Chinese Communist Party.

When a power struggle between the Communists and Chiang Kai-shek's

Nationalists erupted into open warfare in 1927, Mao, proclaiming, "Political power grows out of the barrel of a gun," eagerly joined in the fight. Badly outnumbered by Chiang's army, the Communists were slowly driven out of eastern China and, on the brink of defeat, forced to retreat to the mountains of the northwest in 1934. During this 6,000-mile trek—the famous Long March—Mao emerged as both party chairman and the Communists' top field commander. After arriving at his new headquarters at Yenan Mao remodeled the shattered Red Army into a powerful guerrilla force, and in 1937 began a campaign against the Japanese, who were invading China from their bases in Manchuria. Striking a truce with the Nationalists, Mao's army fought the Japanese for the duration of the Second World War, playing a major role in the Allied campaign for the Far East.

(Opposite) Mao Zedong, the Communist leader who shaped the history of modern China, in military attire.

(Below) Chairman Mao reviews the Red Army's tank corps during the Chinese Civil War. Although he had no formal military training, Mao proved to be an able field commander.

中华人民共和国万岁

At the end of the war, Mao's forces renewed their struggle with the Nationalists for control of China. By striking where Chiang was weak and cultivating the support of the peasants, the Communist guerrillas were able to negate the Nationalist army's vast numerical superiority and by 1948 had turned the tide against Chiang. In January 1949 Peking fell to the Red Army; in October,

A youthful Mao talks with peasants in Yenan Province in 1939. The Communist leader actively courted the support of China's peasants, making them the backbone of his Red Army.

Canton surrendered; and in December the Nationalists fled to Taiwan, leaving Mao as the undisputed leader of the newly created People's Republic of China. In the decades that followed, he

THE DARING AND ERUDITE Augusto Sandino stands among the most important revolutionaries in modern history. His six-year battle against American intervention in Nicaragua was an inspiration to such rebel leaders as Che Guevara and Fidel Castro, and for 50 years after his death he remained a major force in Nicaraguan politics through the actions of his followers, the Sandinistas.

Augusto Cesar Sandino was born in Niquinohomo, Nicaragua, on May 18, 1895, the illegitimate son of a well-to-do landowner and an Indian woman. Raised by his father, Augusto received a good education and later earned a comfortable living as a supervisor on the family farm. He remained there until 1920, when he shot a local man during an argument and fled the country. He spent the following six years working in Honduras, Guatemala, and Mexico, where he became a committed anti-imperialist and Central American nationalist.

Sandino returned to Nicaragua at his father's request in 1926, arriving just before a disputed presidential election between the American-backed Adolfo Díaz and the nationalist Juan Sacasa. When Díaz was declared the winner Sacasa's followers, led by Gen. José Moncada, began an armed insurrection. Sandino immediately offered to help, and after capturing a large supply of arms and ammunition for the rebels' use that December, he was named a general in Moncada's provisional army.

During this time, the Díaz government called upon the United States for assistance, and President Calvin Coolidge responded by dispatching 5,000 marines to the country to restore order. Anxious to bring the fighting to an end, American representatives negotiated a cease-fire between the Díaz and Sacasa camps, offering the marines as a peace-keeping force until the next election, which they would impartially supervise. By May 1927 all of General Moncada's insurgents had agreed to the truce and laid down their arms—except Sandino. Bitter at having foreign troops in his

homeland, he embarked on a campaign of hit-and-run raids against the marines in the Nicaraguan jungles, sorties that became a model for future guerrilla warfare the world over. For six years his "Sandinistas" kept the American and Nicaraguan armed forces at bay, attacking and disappearing at will and taunting his enemies with demands for surrender which typically ended with "Your obedient servant, who wishes to put you in a handsome tomb with flowers, A. C. Sandino."

When Juan Sacasa was finally elected president in 1933 Sandino felt that he could end his fighting and entered into peace negotiations. Following a meeting at Managua on February 21, 1934, he was killed by the order of Nicaragua's infamous chief of security and future dictator Anastasio Somoza.

Augusto Sandino, the wily Nicaraguan rebel who ran circles around the Nicaraguan Army and the U.S. Marines for six years.

Yasir Arafat, militant leader of the Palestine Liberation Organization and chief spokesman of the Palestinian government in exile.

SINCE THE STATE OF ISRAEL was established in 1948, Arab Palestinians have been locked in a struggle with the Israelis for a nation of their own. The central figure in this fight is Yasir Arafat, Chairman of the Palestine Liberation Organization (PLO).

Rahman Abdul Rauf Arafat al-Qudwa al-Husayni was born on August 17, 1929. Although he was raised in Cairo he always considered himself a Palestinian. In the 1940s, while a student in Egypt, he became an ardent Arab nationalist and adopted the name Yasir, after Yasir al Birah, a famous Arab resistance leader. By the time he was 14 he was involved in gunrunning for Arab guerrillas in Gaza, a task he continued to perform during the Israeli War for Independence in 1948.

Following the war he entered Cairo University, where he received a degree in engineering in 1955. During his student days he began to train secretly as a guerrilla, becoming an expert in demolitions and taking part in raids on British installations near the Suez Canal. After his graduation from college he was commissioned a lieutenant in the Egyptian army, with which he saw combat at Port Said and Abu Kabir during the Suez War in October 1956.

In the 1960s Arafat emerged as the chief military and political leader of the Palestinian homeland movement. From his home in Kuwait, where he ran a successful engineering concern, he published the major nationalist organ, *Our Palestine*, and established Al Fatah—an acronym for the Movement for the Liberation of Palestine—sending it on guerrilla raids into Israel. In 1967, after the Arab defeat in the Six-Day War he became chairman of the Palestine Liberation Organization as well. Throughout the 1970s he directed the PLO in a series of terrorist strikes and airline hijackings against Israel and its Western allies. In an effort to garner broader support for his movement in the 1980s he began to distance himself from the PLO's more violent factions like the Abu Nidal group, but he has not firmly renounced terrorism as a means of achieving his goals. He lives in Tunis, where the PLO has its headquarters.

(Opposite) Arafat (left) and an aide survey the war-torn streets of Beirut, Lebanon, in June 1982. The PLO leader takes an active role in the military operations of his followers.

IN THE AFTERMATH OF the Russian Revolution a violent struggle for control of the Soviet Union erupted between Lenin's Bolsheviks, or Reds, and the opposition Whites. The architect of Lenin's victory in this civil war was his ruthless minister of war, Commissar Leon Trotsky.

Trotsky was born Lev Davidovich Bronstein near Elisavetgrad, in the Ukraine, in 1879. He became a revolutionary while a student in Nikolayev, and was sent to Siberia in 1897 for joining a Marxist labor union. After five years he escaped and, under the name of Leon Trotsky—borrowed from one of his jailers—he joined the exiled Lenin in London. After a brief return to Russia in 1905, and another arrest, he fled to the United States.

When the Russian Revolution broke out in March 1917, he quickly returned home and assumed a position of leadership among the Bolsheviks in the revolutionary council (Soviet). That October, he played a key role in engineering Lenin's overthrow of the ruling moderate provisional government. Appointed the first Soviet commissar of foreign affairs, Trotsky quickly negotiated the Treaty of Brest-Litovsk with Germany, ending Russia's participation in the First World War and enabling the Bolsheviks to solidify their control over the government. Redesignated commissar of war, Trotsky organized a Red Army of more than five million and embarked on a long and bitterly fought civil war for control of the country. Although he had no formal military training he proved a master of total warfare, attacking the Whites' economic as well as military bases. Within three years he had crushed all opposition to Lenin's rule.

After Lenin's death in 1924 Trotsky became involved in a power struggle with Joseph Stalin which resulted in Trotsky's expulsion from the Communist Party and exile in 1928. He was assassinated by one of Stalin's agents in Mexico City on August 20, 1940.

(Right) Leon Trotsky (left) in his uniform as Bolshevik minister of war during the Russian Civil War. A ruthless tactician, he utterly crushed the revolt within three years.

(Opposite) This hand-tinted photo was taken while Leon Trotsky was serving as Russian foreign affairs minister in 1917. He was a skilled diplomat who also proved to be a surprisingly good general.

IDI AMIN

Uganda, 1925–

THE HISTORY OF AFRICA since the Second World War has largely been shaped by revolution and revolts. Some have been led by dedicated nationalists such as Jomo Kenyatta; others have been organized by self-serving dictators bent on securing immense personal power and wealth. Among the worst of these was the bloody Ugandan strongman "Big Daddy" Idi Amin.

Idi Amin Dada Oumee was born in Koboko, Uganda, in 1925, a member of the Kakwa tribe. Raised in the isolated farming country of northwestern Uganda, Amin received a scant education which left him functionally illiterate. During the Second World War, at the age of 18, he enlisted in the British East African Rifles and fought in Burma. At the close of the war he joined in the British colonial Fourth Uganda Battalion. After distinguishing himself in the fight against Kenya's Mau Maus between 1953 and 1957, Amin was pro-

moted to sergeant major and admitted to an officer training program. Despite his lack of formal education he proved to be one of Uganda's ablest military commanders, and in 1964, two years after the colony was granted independence, he was appointed deputy chief of the nation's army and air force with the rank of colonel.

When Amin's friend, Dr. Milton Obote, seized power in Uganda in February 1966, he placed Amin in full command of the armed forces, promoting him to major general in 1968. By 1970 a rift had developed between the two, and on January 25, 1971, Amin overthrew Obote, declaring himself president and general (later field marshal). His victory over the authoritarian Obote regime was initially greeted with widespread support, but that rapidly turned to fear and hatred as Amin began solidifying his absolute control over the nation. Within months of assuming office, "Big Daddy" ordered the murder of more than 5,000 members of the rival Acholi

and Langi tribes, beginning a reign of terror that eventually accounted for the deaths of over 150,000 political opponents. Angered over foreign residents' control of Ugandan commerce, he ordered the expulsion of 55,000 Asians, seizing their businesses for himself and his supporters. He then embarked on a campaign designed to humiliate British nationals. This program climaxed in the summer of 1975 when he forced four Englishmen to carry him around an Organization of African Unity rally in a sedan chair.

Amin's oppressive rule was brought to an end in December 1978 when the nation was invaded by a force of 6,000 Ugandan rebels and Tanzanian soldiers. Although Col. Muammar Qaddafi of Libya sent troops to aid the dictator they were not sufficient to quell the popular uprising that ensued, and Amin was forced to flee the country on April 11, 1979. He currently lives in exile in Saudi Arabia.

Ugandan strongman Idi Amin wears his field marshal's uniform for a 1975 appearance at the United Nations. Virtually illiterate, Amin was forced to have someone else read his speech for him.

ERNESTO "CHE" GUEVARA

Cuba, 1928–1967

CHE GUEVARA WAS one of the most influential rebel leaders of the 20th century. A hero of the Cuban Revolution, he led Communist revolts on three continents before his death in action at the age of 39 in 1967.

Ernesto Guevara de la Serna was born to a middle-class family in Misiones, Argentina, on June 14, 1928. Disgusted by the corrupt Argentine government, he became a dedicated Marxist while still in his teens. As a student he vowed to dedicate his life to revolutionary causes, and in 1953, after he received a medical degree from the University of Buenos Aires, he left Argentina to take part in a Communist revolt in Guatemala. There, he adopted the revolutionary nom de guerre Che, the local slang for "pal."

When the revolution in Guatemala failed the following year Che fled to Mexico, where he was introduced to another young exile, Fidel Castro. Joining Castro's July 26 Movement—named for the Cuban's aborted revolution in 1953—Guevara sailed to Cuba with the rest of the movement's guerrilla forces on December 2, 1956, bent on overthrowing the government of Gen. Fulgencio Batista. Proving to be one of Castro's ablest officers, Che was assigned command of half of the small rebel army in July with the rank of comandante, a title he shared only with Castro himself. For the next year and a half he led his insurgents against the government forces in the province of Las Villas, where his successful attack against Santa Clara in December 1958 sealed the victory of Castro's forces over the Batista regime.

After Castro assumed power Che became one of his most trusted advisers and a leading international revolutionary. In 1960 he authored *Guerilla Warfare*, a manual for Third World insurgents. Later he traveled to the Congo and, it is widely believed, Vietnam, to help organize Communist revolts.

On October 7, 1967, he was captured while leading a guerrilla campaign in Bolivia and executed the following day in La Higuera.

The famed doctor turned rebel, Che Guevara. A veritable apostle of revolution, he sparked uprisings from Cuba to the Congo.

GENERAL
EMILIO AGUINALDO
Philippines, 1869–1964

THE HISTORY OF the Philippines over the past hundred years has been the story of a struggle for democracy and freedom from foreign control. The rebel commander Emilio Aguinaldo did more than any other individual to secure the independence of this island nation, leading successive fights against both Spain and the United States at the turn of the century.

Emilio Aguinaldo was born in Kawit, Cavite Province, on March 23, 1869. The son of prominent local attorney and politician Carlos Aguinaldo, Emilio became committed to the Filipino struggle for independence at an early age. In 1895, when he was 26, he joined the secret Katipunan Society, which was dedicated to the overthrow of the Spanish colonial government. When the organization began its revolution against Spain in August 1896, Aguinaldo led the fight in his native Cavite province, decisively defeating the colonial forces there in little over a week and winning promotion to general. Six months later, on March 22, 1897, the convention that established the revolutionary government of the Republic of the Philippines elected him the new nation's first president.

President Aguinaldo continued leading the fight against the Spanish until December 1897, when he agreed to exile himself to Hong Kong in exchange for political reforms, cash indemnities, and a general amnesty for his followers. The Spanish reneged on their promises, however, and at the onset of the Spanish-American War in April 1898 Aguinaldo quickly agreed to America's request that he reorganize the Filipino resistance, ostensibly with the promise of Philippine independence if the Americans won. The general returned to Manila in May and rapidly raised an army of 80,000 which defeated most of the Spanish forces on the Philippines' largest island, Luzon, before the U.S. army's troopships had arrived there.

The diminutive yet inspiring Filipino rebel leader Emilio Aguinaldo, pictured at the time of the Philippine Insurrection in full campaign uniform.

REBELS

At the conclusion of the Spanish-American War on December 10, 1898, Aguinaldo was stunned to find that the United States was annexing, rather than freeing, the Philippines. Feeling betrayed by his former allies, the general issued a Filipino declaration of independence on January 20, 1899, and organized a guerrilla campaign against the American occupation forces serving under Gen. Arthur MacArthur, the father of Douglas MacArthur. Aguinaldo successfully directed the Philippine Insurrection—as it is known in the United States—until his capture by Gen. Frederick Funston on March 23, 1901. To avoid unnecessary bloodshed General Aguinaldo signed a peace agreement on April 19, ending the organized warfare against the Americans; however sporadic fighting continued until 1905 when the last of the insurrectionists were defeated by troops under "Black Jack" Pershing.

Following his surrender Emilio Aguinaldo was released and returned to Cavite province to take up life once more as a private citizen. In 1935 he ran unsuccessfully for president of the Commonwealth of the Philippines. Emilio Aguinaldo died in Manila on February 6, 1964, at the age of 94, having lived long enough to see his dream of a free Philippines become reality.

Aguinaldo (seated bottom row, third from right) and his field commanders from the 1896 revolt against Spain. This photo was taken during the insurrectionists' voluntary exile in Hong Kong.

THE VIETNAMESE GUERRILLA leader Vo Nguyen Giap was one of the century's foremost military commanders. Since 1945 his armies have successively driven the Japanese, the French, and the Americans from Vietnam in a series of extraordinary victories unparalleled since the Second World War.

Vo Nguyen Giap was born in An Xa, Vietnam, on September 1, 1912. An ardent nationalist since his youth, he became a dedicated revolutionary after reading some of Ho Chi Minh's writings. In 1930 he helped found the Vietnamese Communist Party, earning subsequent arrest as a subversive. After his release from jail he entered the University of Hanoi, graduating with a law degree in 1938.

At the outbreak of the Second World War Giap fled to China, where he helped Ho Chi Minh establish the Viet Minh guerrilla movement in 1941. Becoming

the unit's military commander, Giap taught himself the basics of jungle warfare and for the next four years led his troops in a highly effective campaign against the Japanese and Vichy French forces in northern Vietnam. On August 19, 1945, his Viet Minh occupied Hanoi in the wake of the Japanese evacuation, opening the way for Ho to proclaim Vietnam's independence and to establish a provisional government. When the French attempted to reassert their control over the country the following year, Giap organized a guerrilla army of more than 100,000 in opposition. For the next seven years he engaged in a series of hit-and-run raids against the French, finally trapping the main garrison at its base in Dienbienphu. Following a 55-day siege the French surrendered on May 7, 1954, bringing an end to France's rule in Indochina.

The French left behind a nation divided, with Ho's Communists controlling the North and Ngo Dinh Diem's pro-Western

Vo Nguyen Giap, the remarkable self-taught North Vietnamese general who waged a 34-year guerrilla campaign against the armies of Japan, France, America, and South Vietnam.

regime in power in the South. Giap quickly helped organize the Viet Cong, a Communist insurgent army in the South to conduct a guerrilla war against Diem. As the fighting escalated in the early 1960s, American troops were sent to Vietnam to prevent a Communist takeover of the entire nation. In response, Giap mounted a brilliant series of campaigns that significantly contributed to America's withdrawal from South Vietnam in March 1973. Two years later, his forces defeated the South Vietnamese army, ensuring Communist control over all of Vietnam. Since then General Giap, a national hero, has resided in Hanoi.

COMMANDANT-GENERAL

LOUIS BOTHA

South Africa, 1862–1919

DURING THE BOER WAR, from 1899 to 1902, the British army was forced to deploy 500,000 troops in South Africa to counter the daring raids of fewer than 40,000 Boer commandos. The commander responsible for this remarkable guerilla campaign was Louis Botha, the talented general in chief of the Afrikaner forces during most of the war.

Louis Botha was born to a family of Boers—Dutch farmers—near Greytown, South Africa, on September 17, 1862. As a boy Louis moved to the Orange Free State, an area in central South Africa where many Afrikaners—Dutch colonists—settled. There, Botha got his first combat experience serving in a mounted unit during the Zulu War in 1884.

When the Boer War broke out between the English in South Africa and the Afrikaners of the Orange Free State and Transvaal on October 11, 1899, Louis Botha immediately volunteered as an officer in the Boer army. Assigned as aide-de-camp to Gen. Lucas Meyer, Botha demonstrated a natural ability as a tactician and leader in the Boers' opening battles at Laing's Nek and Elandslaagte. When General Meyer became ill during the siege of Ladysmith which followed in November, command of his troops passed to his 37-year-old aide, who was promoted to general. The wily Botha soon stunned the British with brilliant victories at Colenso (December 15, 1899), Spion Kop (January 23, 1900), and Vaal Kranz (February 5), exacting a heavy toll on the forces under Sir Redvers Buller that had been sent to relieve Ladysmith.

When Buller's overwhelming numbers and tactical superiority finally drove the Afrikaners from Ladysmith on February 28, Botha joined his forces with those of Boer commander in chief Petrus Joubert, whom General Botha succeeded as commandant-general on March 21. Following his defeat at the Battle of Bergendal on August 27 the new general in chief realized that his Afrikaners could not win against the British in open combat and that a decisive victory was impossible. He therefore organized his forces into highly mobile bands of mounted riflemen called commandos and embarked upon a campaign of guerrilla warfare designed to force the British government into granting the Boers favorable terms for peace. Botha's hit-and-run raids kept a British army of half a million men at bay for two years until the Treaty of Vereeniging, signed on May 31, 1902, which guaranteed eventual self-rule for the Orange Free State and Transvaal.

After the end of the Boer War Louis Botha remained active in Afrikaner affairs and was elected first president of the newly independent Union of South Africa in 1910. During the First World War he personally led his nation's army to victory against the troops in the neighboring German Southwest Africa. President Botha died in office in Pretoria on August 27, 1919.

Louis Botha, the resourceful South African commando leader who kept the British Army at bay for more than two years during the Boer War.

JOSIP TITO
Yugoslavia, 1892–1980

JOSIP TITO MASTERMINDED what may well have been the most strategically complex guerrilla campaign of the century. The commander of Yugoslavia's Communist partisans during the Second World War, he not only fought the occupying Axis armies but carried on an internal Communist revolution as well, emerging at the war's end as the leader of the new Socialist Federal Republic of Yugoslavia.

Tito was born in Kumrovec, Croatia, then part of the Austro-Hungarian Empire (now Yugoslavia), on May 25, 1892. Christened Josip Broz, he added the surname Tito in 1934 to hide his identity from anti-Communist government officials. A metalworker by trade, he was introduced to the principles of Marxism by fellow union workers while he was in his teens. During the First

World War he was drafted into the Austro-Hungarian army and detailed to the eastern front. There in 1915 he was captured by Russian soldiers. For two years he remained a prisoner of war, but with the outbreak of the Russian Revolution he escaped to join the Bolsheviks in their struggle for control of the nation. He continued to serve in the Red Army until the outbreak of the Russian Civil War the following year, when he made his way back to Yugoslavia. On his return he became an active member of the local Communist Party, which he came to head in 1937.

When Hitler invaded Yugoslavia in April 1941, Tito, following Party dictates from Moscow, remained neutral. Two months later, when the Nazis attacked the USSR and he was finally authorized to act against the Germans, he took to the mountains of Montenegro to form a par-

tisan army with himself as its marshal. Although he received no formal recognition and little aid from the Allies until 1943 he successfully carried on a three-year fight against the occupying armies of Germany, Italy, Hungary, and Bulgaria, driving them from the country by October 1944. In the months that followed he defeated Gen. Draja Mikhailovich's guerrilla forces loyal to Yugoslavia's prewar monarchy, and by V-E Day in May 1945 had become the nation's undisputed leader. In November of that year he proclaimed the country a Communist republic and was subsequently named president for life. Fiercely independent, he was the only Eastern European leader to keep his nation free from Soviet domination in the postwar period. He died in Belgrade on May 4, 1980.

(Right) Josip Tito, the strong-willed partisan leader who kept Yugoslavia independent from both Berlin and Moscow.

(Opposite) The national joy over Tito's victory is delightfully captured in this rare picture of the marshal dancing in the streets of Kola.

FRANCISCO "PANCHO" VILLA

Mexico, 1878–1923

PANCHO VILLA IS AMONG the most colorful and influential men in 20th-century Mexican history. Not only was he a pivotal figure in the revolutions that established modern Mexico, but he also became a national folk hero when he eluded capture by the United States forces under Gen. "Black Jack" Pershing.

Francisco "Pancho" Villa was born to peasant parents in San Juan del Rio, Mexico, on June 5, 1878. Given the name Doroteo Arango, he later took several aliases, the most popular of which was Pancho Villa. Raised in abject poverty in Durango, Mexico, he turned to cattle rustling and robbery as a young man, and soon became one of Mexico's most wanted bandit leaders.

(Opposite) A hand-tinted photo of Pancho Villa, the legendary Mexican bandit and revolutionary.

(Below) Villa (center) and his men on the move in northern Mexico in 1916. Their frequent incursions into United States territory caused the U.S. government to send an army against them but with little success.

As an enemy of the Federal authorities who were trying to arrest him, Villa became a natural ally of Francisco Madero in the latter's struggle to overthrow President Porfirio Díaz. Appointed a colonel in Madero's revolutionary army, he led his forces in a daring raid against Juárez on May 11, 1911, capturing the city and securing Madero's position as the new president. When Madero was assassinated two years later in a coup led by Vitoriano Huerta, Villa quickly reorganized his Army of the North and became one of the most important leaders of the anti-Huerta faction. His highly mobile mounted troops, called *villistas*, triumphed over the new president's army in northern Mexico in the Battle of Zacatecas on June 23, 1913, and then began a campaign to the south. By December they had captured Mexico City in conjunction with revolutionaries under Venustiano Carranza and Emiliano Zapata, placing control of the government in the hands of the three rebel leaders.

The following spring Villa lost his position of national leadership in a power struggle with Carranza and was driven back to his headquarters in Durango.

There he resumed life as a bandit, raiding American border villages and mining camps as well as Mexican towns. On March 9, 1916, his men massacred dozens of unarmed Americans in a gruesome attack on Columbus, New Mexico, prompting the United States to dispatch an army unit under Gen. John J. Pershing to capture the brigands. Villa's maneuverability and superior knowledge of the terrain enabled him to elude the Americans, however, and Pershing's troops withdrew the following year.

In 1920 the Mexican government reached an agreement with Villa under which he halted his raids in return for a ranch in Canutillo and his appointment to general of the Mexican army. He was subsequently assassinated in Parral, Mexico, on June 20, 1923, by the followers of Álvaro Obregón, who feared that he would oppose their leader's candidacy for president in the upcoming elections.

The bandit leader Villa was looked upon as a hero by the common people of Mexico—especially the children.

GENERAL OF THE ARMY
RAOUL SALAN
France, 1899–1984

IN 1961 THE FRENCH armed forces in Algeria, still smarting from their losses in Indochina and the Suez, mutinied to protest plans granting independence to the colony. The revolt was planned by a clandestine group of disaffected army officers led by the most highly decorated French soldier of the 20th century, Gen. Raoul Salan.

Raoul Albin Louis Salan was born in Roquecourbe, France, on June 10, 1899. He entered the French Military Academy at Saint-Cyr during the First World War, and after just one year's study was commissioned a lieutenant in 1917. A fearless fighter, he had won the Croix de Guerre by war's end, the first of 36 medals and campaign citations that he would receive during his long military career.

Following the Armistice, Salan served in Syria, Indochina, and Central Africa. During the Second World War he initially supported the Vichy regime, but after two years he joined the Free French and fought with distinction in the Allied invasion of southern France, winning promotion to brigadier general. After the war he served as the French commander in chief in Indochina and Algeria and rose to the five-star rank of Général d'Armée.

In December 1958 Salan was removed from command in Algeria by President Charles de Gaulle shortly after he returned to power. Embittered Salan retired from the service and went to Spain, where he took a leading role in establishing the Organisation de l'Armée Secrète (OAS), an underground group of officers dedicated to keeping Algeria a French possession. When de Gaulle announced a referendum on Algerian independence in 1961, Salan returned to Algeria and led the OAS commanders in a revolt against the French president on April 22. Although the coup was stopped within two days by troops loyal to de Gaulle, the OAS members carried on a terrorist campaign against proindependence officials until Salan was captured on April 20, 1962. He was swiftly sentenced to life imprisonment for his role in the revolt but was released in a general amnesty six years later, and in 1982 his military pension and decorations—but not his rank—were restored. He died in Paris on July 3, 1984.

General Raoul Salan, the veteran French Army commander who led the abortive 1961 officers' revolt in Algeria. On his chest he displays the rows of ribbons that marked him as France's most highly decorated soldier.

The 29-year-old Ho at the Versailles Peace Conference in 1919. After trying in vain to get an agreement on the independence of Indochina there he turned to more radical methods to achieve this goal.

paign that succeeded in harassing the Japanese.

The Allied victory left Ho in effective control of the nation, and after proclaiming a "people's government" he was elected president in January 1946. When the French attempted to reassert their rule over Indochina later that year he declared a war of independence, and in a classic guerrilla campaign drove them from Vietnam in May 1954. Under the Geneva peace agreement that ended the war, the country was partitioned into North Vietnam (Communist) and South Vietnam (non-Communist), but free elections to establish a national government were to be held within two years. However, the pro-Western government in the South blocked a vote, and Ho embarked on another guerrilla campaign, which escalated into a full-scale war when the United States sent troops to the South's assistance in the early 1960s. Ho prosecuted the struggle relentlessly, and at the time of his death in Hanoi on September 3, 1969, had firmly laid the groundwork for the victory that his forces ultimately won over the South in 1975.

BETWEEN 1941 AND 1974, the North Vietnamese people fought a series of guerrilla wars against the Japanese, the French, and the American-backed South Vietnamese for control of their country. The political and military leader of these struggles was Ho Chi Minh, one of the most effective Communist insurgents of the 20th century.

Ho was born in Kim Lien, Vietnam, on May 19, 1890. Named Nguyen That Thanh at birth, he took the name Ho Chi Minh—"Most Enlightened One"— during the Second World War. He started his long career as a revolutionary at the age of nine by smuggling messages for his father, an anti-French activist. In 1912, after finishing his schooling in Vietnam, he traveled around the world to continue his political education. He spent several years in France, where he became a Communist Party leader, and several years in Moscow, where he studied revolutionary tactics.

Upon leaving the Soviet Union in 1925, Ho traveled to China to train guerrillas for the Chinese Communist Party. While there, he began recruiting Vietnamese exiles for a liberation movement, organizing them into the Vietnamese Communist Party in 1930, with himself as chairman. At the outbreak of the Sec-

ond World War he established a guerrilla unit, the Viet Minh, to fight the Japanese and Vichy French in his homeland. Returning to Vietnam after an absence of 30 years, Chairman Ho appointed a young disciple, Vo Nguyen Giap, as his field commander and together they directed a jungle cam-

An oil portrait of Ho Chi Minh, the single-minded leader who dedicated his life to ending foreign control over Vietnam.

COMANDANTE

FIDEL CASTRO

Cuba, 1926–

FOR SOME THREE DECADES Fidel Castro has been the Western Hemisphere's most influential revolutionary leader. Ruling Cuba with an iron hand since 1959, he has transformed his country into a totalitarian Communist state and taken an active role in assisting Marxist revolutions throughout Central America and Africa.

Fidel Castro Ruz was born on his family's sugar plantation near Biran, Cuba, on August 13, 1926. A highly intelligent young man, he entered the University of Havana Law School directly from high school in 1945. While a student there, he became interested in the anti-imperialist movement and the movement for student social reform and joined the radical Unión Insurreccional Revolucionaria. In 1947 he took part in an unsuccessful attempt to overthrow the Dominican Republic's dictator Rafael Trujillo, and the following year he participated in anti-American riots in Bogota, Colombia.

After receiving his law degree in 1950 Castro opened a practice in Havana and became active in liberal politics. He vehemently opposed Gen. Fulgencio Batista's seizure of the Cuban government on March 10, 1952, and shortly thereafter organized an armed resistance against the dictator. On July 26, 1953, he launched a counterrevolution in Oriente province but it failed, and he was sentenced to 15 years in prison.

Released from jail during a general amnesty in 1955, Castro left the country for Mexico, where he began organizing forces for another attempt to overthrow Batista. On December 2, 1956, he led members of his "July 26 Movement," including the Argentine revolutionary Ernesto "Che" Guevara, back to Cuba to begin a guerrilla war against the

Castro (center) served as both military and political leader of the Cuban Revolution, directing a highly effective two-year guerrilla campaign against the Battista government.

government. Although his provisional army never numbered more than 1,000 soldiers he kept Batista's army of 30,000 at bay for two years, winning widespread support in one of the most successful insurgent campaigns in history. On December 31, 1958, Batista fled the country and his army surrendered to the rebels; the following day Castro seized power in Havana, declaring himself *comandante* of the Cuban armed forces and, later, premier. After purging the country of Batista supporters and other opponents he began a campaign designed to turn Cuba into a socialist state. He nationalized private property, assumed control of schools, and ruthlessly suppressed dissent. After defeating the American-backed Bay of Pigs invasion in April 1961, Castro declared himself a Marxist, and in 1965 made the Communist Party Cuba's official political organization.

Since assuming power Castro has supported numerous Communist "people's liberation" movements in Latin America and Africa, supplying them with Cuban technical advisers and troops. The changes that have come elsewhere with *glasnost* and *perestroika* have had no effect on Castro, and under him Cuba remains an absolute Communist dictatorship.

(Above right) Castro gives a bearhug to Nikita Khrushchev (right) at the United Nations during the latter's historic visit to New York in September 1960. Although the Russian leader was Castro's staunchest ally, this was the first time the two men actually met.

(Right) In a scene reminiscent of a rock concert, a crowd of adoring Havana schoolgirls mob the Cuban president in January 1959 before he delivers a speech on the importance of sports. In his youth, Castro was an avid baseball player.

(Opposite) Fidel Castro, the unwavering hard-line Communist dictator of Cuba, addresses a Havana crowd in February 1977. He wears the uniform of a comandante of the Cuban armed forces.

GENERALISSIMO
FRANCISCO FRANCO
Spain, 1892–1975

FROM 1936 TO 1939, SPAIN was involved in a bloody civil war pitting leftist Loyalists against fascist Nationalists. The victor in this struggle was Generalissimo Francisco Franco, the commander of the Nationalist forces and dictator of Spain for nearly 40 years.

Francisco Paulino Hermenegildo Teódulo Franco y Bahamonde was born in El Ferrol, Spain, on December 4, 1892. He entered the Spanish Academia de Infantería in 1907, and upon his graduation three years later was commissioned a lieutenant. His career rose meteorically when he was detailed to the colony of Spanish Morocco to fight the Rif (Berber) tribes. In 1916 he won promotion to major for his bravery in the Battle of El Biutz; in 1923 he was appointed commander in chief of the Spanish Foreign Legion; and in 1926, at age 33, he was named the army's youngest brigadier general.

Franco returned to Spain in 1927 to head the National Military Academy. Assigned to quell a miners' strike in Asturias in 1934, he revealed himself to be a ruthless authoritarian by ordering the execution of 2,000 of the laborers who were suspected of being Marxists. Marked thereafter as one of the army's staunchest anti-Communists, he was invited to take a leading role in a right-wing coup being planned by some fellow officers. He accepted, and shortly after the revolt broke out on July 17, 1936, was named commander of the Nationalist forces with the title generalissimo. Although he hoped to seize control of the government quickly, the struggle evolved into a full-scale civil war that lasted for nearly three years. With heavy assistance from Hitler and Mussolini, Franco finally emerged as the victor, capturing the capital city of Madrid on March 29, 1939.

Named *caudillo*, dictator for life, Generalissimo Franco proved to be an astute political leader as well as a masterful military commander. Although he owed a tremendous debt of thanks to Nazi Germany and fascist Italy for their aid during the civil war he managed to keep Spain neutral during the Second World War, and after the Axis powers were defeated he successfully allied himself with the United States. He served as head of state until his death in Madrid on November 20, 1975.

Generalissimo Francisco Franco, the autocratic professional soldier who led the Nationlist forces to victory in the Spanish Civil War. Even before this triumph he was widely regarded as Spain's most outstanding military commander.

REBELS

Franco (center) oversees Nationalist operations in Catalonia in January 1939, a few months before sealing his victory over the Loyalists with the capture of Madrid.

MUAMMAR QADDAFI

Libya, 1942–

MUAMMAR QADDAFI IS one of the most powerful revolutionary leaders in the world today. The Chairman of the Libyan Arab Republic and commander in chief of its armed forces, he has used his nation's oil wealth to actively support rebel movements and terrorists throughout the Third World.

Muammar Abu Meniar el-Qaddafi was born in the desert south of Sirte, Libya, in 1942; the exact date is unknown. The son of a poor Bedouin, he lived in his family's remote desert camp until he went away to school at the age of nine. It was while he was a student in the secondary school at Sebha that Qaddafi, inspired by the speeches of Egyptian President Gamal Abdul Nasser, became a committed Arab nationalist. A natural leader, he organized his fellow students into revolutionary study groups at Sebha and continued the practice at the University of Libya, from which he received a history degree in 1963.

Following his graduation Qaddafi entered the Libyan Military Academy at Benghazi, where he found many of the cadets were sympathetic to his anti-Western nationalism. Commissioned a lieutenant in the Libyan army in 1965, he began laying the groundwork for an overthrow of the Libyan monarch, King Idris, whom he considered a pawn of the West. Within four years he and his followers had won control of the army, and on the morning of September 1, 1969, he seized power in a carefully orchestrated coup d'état. Assuming the reins of government as chairman of the ruling Revolutionary Council, Qaddafi declared himself commander in chief of the Libyan armed forces with the rank of colonel. (In 1976 he promoted himself to the rank of major general but for some reason prefers to use his revolutionary title of colonel.) Qaddafi soon began implementing his long dreamed of plans for a Libya for Libyans, nationalizing foreign banks and petroleum companies and closing the country's British and American military bases. In 1970 he seized the private assets of Libya's Italian and Jewish residents, driving them from the country.

Since assuming power Colonel Qaddafi has given heavy support to a wide variety of terrorist organizations and regimes, including the Palestine Liberation Organization's Black September faction, the Irish Republican Army, and Uganda's Idi Amin. On April 15, 1986, his government's involvement in a nightclub explosion in West Germany that killed a U.S. serviceman and wounded others precipitated a retaliatory American bombing raid on his headquarters in Tripoli, but he escaped unharmed and remains in firm control of his government.

Col. Muammar Qaddafi of Libya, the fanatical Arab nationalist and revolutionary.

Qaddafi (seated center) signs an agreement with Anwar Sadat of Egypt (left) and Hafez Assad of Syria in 1971, creating a Federation of Arab Republics from their three nations. After the Federation failed, the erratic Libyan dictator attacked his former ally, Egypt.

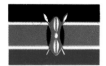

JOMO KENYATTA

Kenya, ca. 1891–1978

IN THE EARLY 1950s the British colony of Kenya was rocked by a native rebellion against foreign control. Leadership of this uprising is generally credited to one of Africa's leading freedom fighters, the father of an independent Kenya, Jomo Kenyatta.

Kenyatta was born in Ngenda, Kenya, in 1891; he was never sure of the date, although October 20 of that year is sometimes given. A member of the Kikuyu tribe, he was named Kamau wa Ngengi at birth, and later christened Johnstone Kamau by Scottish missionaries. He adopted the name Jomo Kenyatta in the 1920s, taking his first name from the Kikuyu word for "burning spear," and his surname from the beaded belt, or *kenyatta*, he often wore.

Kenyatta became active in Kenyan politics in the early 1920s as a member of the nationalist Kikuyu Central Association. By the end of the decade he had become the nation's most influential

spokesman for freedom from colonial rule. Sent abroad to study and garner support for his cause, he spent most of the 1930s at universities in Britain and the USSR. Although he remained in the United Kingdom through the Second World War, he kept in close contact with his followers back home, and upon his return to Kenya in 1946 was elected chairman of the Kenya African Union, the successor to the banned Kikuyu Association.

Shortly after Kenyatta's return to his homeland a violent nationalist organization, the Mau Mau, was formed to oppose British rule. Aiming their initial raids at natives who assisted the colonial government, the Mau Mau killed thousands between 1948 and 1952, when a full-scale uprising began. Although Kenyatta always denied any connection with the Mau Mau, he was the unchallenged leader of Kenya's nationalist movement, and it seems improbable that he did not have some link to that largely Kikuyu organization.

In any case, he was arrested on October 20, 1952, by colonial authorities on charges of inciting the insurrection. Convicted and jailed for nine years, he became a national hero.

After Kenyatta was released in August 1961 he continued his work for national independence, and when it was finally achieved on December 11, 1963, he was triumphantly swept into office first as prime minister, then as president. He died in office in Nairobi on August 22, 1978.

Jomo "Burning Spear" Kenyatta, the driving force behind Kenya's independence movement.

EMILIANO ZAPATA

Mexico, 1879–1919

DURING THE EARLY YEARS of the 20th century, Mexico was wracked by a series of revolutions centering on the demand for land by the nation's large class of tenant farmers, the peons. Their greatest champion was the self-taught revolutionary and national hero Emiliano Zapata.

Emiliano Zapata was born in Anenecuilo, Mexico, on August 8, 1879. The son of a businessman, Zapata was not himself a peon but was raised among them in the predominantly agrarian Morelos district, where the living conditions convinced him of the need for sweeping reforms. He became the peasants' spokesman in the area and was briefly drafted into the Mexican army as punishment for his radical statements on their behalf. In the early 1900s, as public opinion grew against the dictatorial Mexican President Porfirio Díaz, Zapata started organizing the men of Morelos into a revolutionary army. He proved a natural tactician as well as an inspiring leader, and when the revolt against Díaz headed by Francisco Madero broke out in March 1911 he was appointed *Supremo* (Supreme Chief) of the Revolutionary Movement of the South. By the end of May his troops had defeated the government forces at Yautepec, Cuautla, and Cuernavaca, playing a key role in Madero's subsequent victory.

When Madero was overthrown by Vitoriano Huerta in 1913, Zapata entered into a campaign of guerrilla warfare against the new repressive administration. By July 1914 he had fought his way to the outskirts of Mexico City, forcing Huerta to flee. Four months later, when the revolutionaries' victory was complete, he entered the capital in triumph with fellow army commanders Pancho Villa and Venustiano Carranza, and the three established a provisional government. By the following spring Zapata, like Villa, was ousted from the new government by Carranza and his followers. Once again, Zapata entered into a protracted guerrilla war against the government. After a four-year stalemate the struggle was finally resolved when Carranza's men assassinated Zapata at a peace conference in Chinameca, on April 10, 1919. Zapata's reforms were reinstituted following Carranza's demise, and he is today regarded as a martyr to the cause of Mexican liberty.

Emiliano Zapata, the champion of the Mexican peasants. The colorful rebel leader's sombrero, bandoliers, and bushy moustache have become the symbols of Mexico's revolutionaries.

ZHOU ENLAI
China, 1898–1976

PREMIER ZHOU ENLAI is widely recognized as the most influential diplomat in the history of Communist China. Less commonly known, but no less important, is his major role as second-in-command of Mao Zedong's Red Army during its many years of fighting with Chiang Kai-shek's Nationalists.

Zhou Enlai was born in Hwaian, China, in 1898. Although he was the son of an imperial government bureaucrat, Zhou was disillusioned by the Manchu court's concessions to the West and became a militant nationalist. He joined the Socialist movement in 1917 while a student in Japan, and shortly after his return to China two years later was arrested for being a leftist agitator. Upon his release in 1920 he fled to France, where he became an active corresponding member of the newly founded Chinese Communist Party.

After finishing his Marxist studies Zhou went back to China in 1922 to join Sun Yat-sen, then cooperating with the Communists. In 1924 he taught at the Whampoa Military Academy, which was then under Communist control. A born leader, he was soon appointed head of the Party's Kwangtung Military Committee, then commanded by Chiang Kai-shek. In 1927, two years after Sun's death, fighting broke out between the Communists and Chiang's Nationalist forces in Shanghai. During this battle, Zhou emerged as one of the Communists' top commanders. By 1931 he had become second-in-command of the Red Army with the rank of general, playing a leading role in the Communists' continuing guerrilla war against Chiang and in the Long March retreat that followed in 1934.

After the Japanese invaded China from Manchuria in 1937, Zhou negotiated a truce between the warring Chinese armies, thereby enabling them to present a united front against Japan. Throughout the Second World War he served as the Communists' chief liaison with Chiang Kai-shek, an assignment that signaled his transition from field commander to diplomat. As a result of his new role, Zhou helped plan overall strategy during the civil war between the Nationalists and the Communists but he did not lead troops into combat. Following the Communists' victory in 1949, Zhou was named premier and foreign minister. In the ensuing years he played an important role in the negotiations that ended the Korean War and the French presence in Indochina. He died in Peking on January 8, 1976, second only to Chairman Mao Zedong in the Communist hierarchy.

(Right) Zhou Enlai, the able diplomat and general who played a key role in the founding of the People's Republic of China.

(Opposite) Zhou primarily built his reputation on his skills as a diplomat. Here he is seen with President Richard Nixon celebrating one of his greatest triumphs, the renewal of Chinese relations with the United States in 1972.

Israeli Defense Minister Moshe Dayan peers out from a bunker during the Yom Kippur War. Although he was surprised by the Arab offensive, he quickly led his armed forces to victory in a series of brilliant counterattacks.

LEADERS OF MEN

GEORGE S. PATTON, JR.

United States, 1885–1945

WITH THE POSSIBLE exception of Confederate Gen. Jeb Stuart, "Blood and Guts" George S. Patton was probably the most colorful general in American history; he was certainly one of the best. Brash and egomaniacal, he inspired his soldiers to superhuman efforts during the Second World War with his flamboyant style and legendary pep talks.

George Smith Patton, Jr. was born in San Gabriel, California, on November 11, 1885. Raised in rural California, where he became an expert horseman and hunter, Patton was inspired to seek a military career through the stories of his ancestors, who included a Revolutionary War general and a Confederate colonel. He entered the Virginia Military Academy in 1903, the third generation of his family to attend the school, and transferred to the U.S. Military Academy the following year. Upon his graduation in 1909 Patton was commissioned a lieutenant in the cavalry. After studying cavalry tactics in France and designing the last saber used by mounted troops in the U.S. Army, Patton was detailed as Gen. "Black Jack" Pershing's aide in the Mexican Border campaign of 1916. There, he gained his initial experience in mechanized warfare by leading the first motorized patrol in history to engage in combat. The following year, during the First World War, Patton organized the AEF's fledgling tank corps, playing a key role in the army's transition from horse cavalry to mechanized armor. Commanding the 304th Tank Brigade in the St. Mihiel and Meuse-Argonne offensives in 1918, he won the Distinguished Service Cross and promotion to colonel for his bravery at the front.

After the war Patton served in numerous tank and cavalry posts, becoming the army's leading proponent of mechanized armor and rising to the rank of major general. Shortly after the United States entered the Second World War, he was named commander of the First Armored Corps. Assigned to head the U.S. invasion of Morocco, he directed the landings near Casablanca on November 8, 1942, and succeeded to command of the U.S. Second Army Corps in Tunisia the following March. After the Allied victory in North Africa he led the American Seventh Army on its successful campaign in Sicily in July 1943, capturing Palermo and Messina in just 38 days.

After securing Sicily Patton, who had been promoted to lieutenant general, was severely reprimanded for slapping a shellshocked soldier in a base hospital. Transferred to Britain, he was given command in March 1944 of the U.S. Third Army, which was then preparing for the Allied invasion of Europe. Patton's troops landed in France a few weeks after D-Day that June and spearheaded the American advance south and east of Normandy. His tanks raced through France, stopping only when they ran out of gas. After playing a decisive role in turning back the Nazi counteroffensive at the Battle of the Bulge in December, Patton's units crossed the Rhine in March 1945 and by the end of the war had smashed their way through central Germany to Czechoslovakia.

For his role in conquering Hitler's armies Patton was promoted to full general in April 1945. At the close of hostilities he was appointed military governor of Bavaria but was removed from office in September for advocating the reinstatement of former Nazis in government positions. He died in Heidelberg, Germany, as a result of an automobile accident on December 21, 1945.

(Opposite) George S. Patton reveled in the gruff "Blood and Guts" image reflected in this 1942 picture. Despite his histrionics—or perhaps because of them—he was one of the finest generals of the 20th century.

(Above) Patton (left center) landing in Morocco in 1942. His success in this, the first American campaign of the war, paved the way for his subsequent command assignments in Tunisia and Sicily.

(Right) General Patton (right) looks typically spit-and-polish in his dress uniform as he escorts French Governor Gen. Auguste Nogues around Morocco early in 1943.

CHIANG KAI-SHEK

China, 1887–1975

CHIANG KAI-SHEK IS one of the pivotal figures of modern Chinese history. The leader of Nationalist China for 50 years, he unified the nation under his rule in the 1930s only to redivide it in a power struggle with Mao Zedong's Communists after the Second World War.

Chiang Kai-shek was born in Fenghua, China, on October 31, 1887, the son of a poor merchant. He entered the Paoting Military Academy in 1906, and after a year was sent to Japan for further studies. While in Japan, he became a disciple of the exiled Chinese revolutionary Dr. Sun Yat-sen. When Sun's Kuomintang (Nationalist) Party began its revolt against Manchu rule in October 1911, Chiang served as a field commander, scoring an impressive victory against the imperial forces in Hangchow in 1912. By 1921 he had risen to the position of Sun's chief of staff and senior military adviser.

After Sun's death in 1925 Chiang became the leader of the Nationalists, who then controlled only southern China. Anxious to expand his power, the Generalissimo led an army of Nationalist troops on a campaign that successfully unified the nation under his rule in 1928. When his authority was challenged by the Communists he embarked on a six-year campaign against Mao Zedong and his supporters, finally driving them from their base of power in central China in 1934. This victory over the Communists, although temporary, solidified Chiang's power as political leader of China and marked the high point of his military career.

The Generalissimo's successes as a commander were rapidly reversed during the Second Sino-Japanese War which followed in 1937. Preoccupied during his struggle with the Communists, he had allowed the Japanese to seize Manchuria in 1932, but when they moved into eastern China five years later he was compelled to take action. Woefully ill-equipped to face the modern Japanese army, Chiang lost badly in the east and was forced to retreat far

inland to Chungking in 1938. With heavy aid from the United States and occasional support in the north from Mao's Red Army, with which he had established an uneasy truce, he was able to maintain control over western China until the end of the Second World War, but his campaigns against the Japanese made little or no progress.

After the Japanese surrender in 1945, civil war erupted between Chiang's

Nationalists and Mao's Communists. By 1948 Chiang was no longer able to contain the Red Army, and after losing Mukden and Peking to Mao's forces he fled to Taiwan on January 21, 1949, where he established a Nationalist government in exile. He remained in power in the capital city of Taipei until his death on April 5, 1975, still harboring dreams of a return to the mainland.

Chiang Kai-shek, the strong-willed generalissimo of Nationalist China for nearly 50 years. A better politician than military man, he was unable to defeat the Japanese during World War II or Mao Zedong's Communists afterward.

FREDERICK FUNSTON

United States, 1865–1917

ALTHOUGH HE IS scarcely known today, Gen. Frederick Funston was considered second only to "Black Jack" Pershing among the officers of the U. S. Army in the years before the First World War. Bold and resourceful, Funston became a national hero when he captured the Filipino rebel leader Emilio Aguinaldo during the Philippine Insurrection.

"Fighting Fred" Funston was born in New Carlisle, Ohio, on November 9, 1865, the son of Union Army soldier and politician Edward Funston. Rejected by West Point because of his poor scores on the entrance exam, Frederick became a botanist with the U.S. Department of Agriculture, where he was able to indulge his thirst for excitement with expeditions to Death Valley and the Yukon.

When the Cuban insurrection against Spain broke out in 1895 Funston, who still had hopes of a military career, offered his services to the revolutionary forces as an artillery officer. Although he later claimed that his only formal training lay in having once observed the firing of a salute at a Kansas county fair, "Fighting Fred" proved himself a talented officer in Cuba and returned to the United States as a lieutenant colonel in January 1898.

At the outbreak of the Spanish-American War three months later Funston, by then a national celebrity, was commissioned colonel of the 20th Kansas Volunteers. Although the regiment did not arrive at its post in the Philippines until after the war with Spain had ended (much to Funston's disappointment), the unit was assigned to active duty with the American forces combatting the native insurrection led by Emilio Aguinaldo. "Fighting Fred" soon rose to prominence, winning promotion to brigadier general and the Congressional Medal of Honor at age 36 for his fearless capture of a strategic bridgehead during the Battle of Calumpit against the Filipinos on April 27, 1899.

Funston's most important role in the Philippine Insurrection was the capture of Aguinaldo himself in March 1901. When intercepted rebel correspondence revealed that the rebel leader had established his headquarters in the remote village of Palanan, Funston devised a daring plan to snare him. Dis-

"Fighting Fred" Funston, mastermind behind the capture of Filipino rebel leader Emilio Aguinaldo and one of the U.S. Army's top officers at the turn of the century.

guising a band of loyal Filipino soldiers as rebels, Funston had them bring him and a handful of other American officers to Palanan as prisoners. Once within the rebel camp, they overwhelmed Aguinaldo's bodyguard and on March 25, 1901, had him imprisoned on board a U.S. Navy gunboat waiting offshore. The capture of Aguinaldo brought an end to the Philippine Insurrection.

On returning to the United States, "Fighting Fred" was greeted as a hero and placed in charge of the army forces in California, where he acted as military governor following the San Francisco earthquake in 1906. In 1914 he was ordered to capture Vera Cruz, Mexico, in a show of strength against Victoriano Huerta's government, an action that earned him promotion to major general on November 17.

General Funston died in San Antonio, Texas, on February 19, 1917, and was buried with full military honors in the Presidio, San Francisco. The death of this remarkable commander was considered a major loss to the nation's war effort when the United States entered the Great War two months later.

MATTHEW RIDGWAY

United States, 1895–

THE KOREAN CONFLICT has often been called America's forgotten war, and in many ways its Allied commander, Matthew Ridgway, is America's forgotten general. A first-rate field officer in the Second World War and Korea, Ridgway has been overshadowed by better known colleagues such as Omar Bradley and Douglas MacArthur, depriving him of the popular recognition he deserves.

Matthew Bunker Ridgway was born in Fort Monroe, Virginia, on March 3, 1895, the son of Col. Thomas Ridgway. Raised in army posts, he naturally gravitated toward a military career, graduating from the U.S. Military Academy as a

lieutenant of infantry in 1917. He spent the First World War on duty in Texas, after which he served as an instructor at West Point and in posts throughout the United States, the Far East, and Central America.

When the United States entered the Second World War Ridgway was promoted to major general and assigned command of the newly organized 82nd Airborne Division, leading the unit in its first assault during the invasion of Sicily in June 1943. Three months later, at the outset of the Italian campaign, he performed what he felt was the greatest service of his career by forestalling a disastrously premature attack on Rome in favor of the Allied landing at Salerno.

The following year he led his 6,000 paratroopers in securing the Utah beachhead during the Normandy invasion and won promotion to lieutenant general with command of the 18th Army Corps. After spearheading the Allied advance in Denmark in April 1945, he was dispatched to the Philippines to assume command of airborne operations against Japan, but the war ended before he saw action in the Pacific.

Ridgway spent the next five years in administrative posts, rising to the position of Army Deputy Chief of Staff by June 1950. When Chinese Communist troops drove the Allied forces in Korea

south of the 38th parallel in November he was detailed to the front as commander of the dispirited Eighth Army. His frontline style of leadership made him popular with the troops, and within two months he had not only restored morale but had also led his forces in a new offensive which recaptured Seoul and forced the much larger North Korean army into retreat. Promoted to full general in April 1951 he succeeded Douglas MacArthur as commander in chief of the Allied forces, stabilizing his troop line along the demilitarized zone. Two months later he opened the peace talks that finally brought an end to the hostilities on July 27, 1953. Following his tour of duty in Korea, Ridgway served as supreme commander of NATO and Army Chief of Staff. He retired from the service on June 30, 1955, and at age 95 lives on as the army's Grand Old Man.

(Right) Gen. Matthew Ridgway, commander of the Allied forces in Korea and one of the toughest fighting generals in the American Army, standing in front of his personal B-17. The plane's name, "Hi Penny," is a message to his wife, Penny Anthony Ridgway.

(Opposite) Ridgway (center) at the front in Korea, March 1951. The general always traveled heavily armed; his men nicknamed him "old iron tit" after his practice of carrying a live hand grenade clipped to his vest.

JACQUES LECLERC

France, 1902–1947

DURING THE SECOND World War, France's early surrender restricted the Free French to mainly underground resistance. A notable exception was the force directed by France's most aggressive field commander during the war, Gen. Jacques Leclerc. For three years Leclerc led a hardhitting campaign by French colonial troops in central Africa, and then crowned his wartime achievements by commanding the French forces that recaptured Paris in 1944.

Jacques-Philippe Leclerc was born at Belloy-Saint-Leonard, France, on November 28, 1902. The scion of a titled Gallic family, he was baptized Philippe Marie, vicomte de Hauteclocque, but took the *nom de guerre* Jacques Leclerc during the Second World War to protect family members living in occupied territory. A graduate of the French military academy at Saint-Cyr in 1924, Leclerc developed a reputation as a fine officer during his service in Morocco, and by the beginning of the Second World War he had advanced to a position on the general staff with the rank of captain.

During the German invasion of France in May 1940 Captain Leclerc was assigned to field command with the Fourth Infantry and was twice captured by Hitler's forces, narrowly escaping both times. After Pétain's capitulation on June 21 he made his way to Britain, where he joined Gen. Charles de Gaulle's Free French movement.

Promoted to colonel, Leclerc was given the key assignment of rallying the French colonial forces in Central Africa to the support of de Gaulle rather than Marshal Pétain's Vichy government. By August, after he had been in Africa for little more than a month, the intrepid colonel had succeeded in winning Cameroon, Chad, and the Congo to the Free French cause. By the end of the year his troops, which had secured all of French Equatorial Africa for the Allies, had begun harassing the Italian forces in southern Libya, earning their leader promotion to brigadier general. The indomitable Frenchman culminated his North African campaign in December 1942 by leading a 1,500-mile march across the deserts of Niger and Libya to join the final Allied assault on Erwin Rommel's Afrikakorps in Tunisia.

General Leclerc changed his theater of operations from Africa to Europe in

August 1944. Joining in the Allied invasion of southern France he was assigned command of the French Second Armored Division, which he proudly led into Paris on August 23, accepting the German garrison's surrender the next day. The general followed this triumph by liberating Strasbourg and Bordeaux in November and leading the column that captured Hitler's retreat at Berchtesgaden in April 1945.

With the defeat of Germany in May, General Leclerc was dispatched to the Far East as French commander in chief. After ratifying the Japanese surrender for de Gaulle's government in September he turned his attention to the rebellion that Ho Chi Minh was fostering in French Indo-China. The commander recognized that France's position in Southeast Asia was untenable and recommended a negotiated withdrawal, but his farsighted appraisal was rejected and he was recalled. Reassigned in July 1946 as inspector-general of French forces in North Africa with the rank of full general, Jacques Leclerc died in a plane crash near Colon Bechar, Algeria, on his 45th birthday, November 28, 1947. In 1952 he was posthumously promoted to marshal of France.

(Opposite) Marshal Jacques Leclerc standing before the Arc de Triomphe in Paris.

(Right) Leclerc (right) and two of his aides during the Allied campaign against Rommel's Afrikakorps in Tunisia in 1943. The French commander led his men on a 1,500 mile trek across central Africa to join in the attack.

WILLIAM MITCHELL

United States, 1879–1936

GEN. BILLY MITCHELL endured one of the most tragic careers in American military history. The individual most responsible for the development of U.S. airpower—indeed, for modern military air tactics—he was an unceasing advocate for American military preparedness and for this he was court-martialed rather than given the top command he deserved.

William Mitchell, the son of Wisconsin Congressman (later Senator) John L. Mitchell, was born in Nice, France, on December 29, 1879. Raised in Wisconsin, he dropped out of George Washington University at the outbreak of the Spanish-American War in 1898 to enlist in the army. Commissioned a lieutenant in the Signal Corps, he distinguished himself in Cuba and the Philippines, where he served during the Filipino Insurrection. He continued to build a fine reputation as an officer after his return to the United States in 1901; by 1912 at the age of 32 he had become

(Opposite) Gen. Billy Mitchell, the uncompromising advocate of American air power who built the Army Air Force into a world class combat unit.

(Below) Mitchell (right) at his headline-making 1926 court-martial. Demoted for his outspoken opinions about American military preparedness, he engineered the trial to provide a public forum for his views.

the youngest member of the General Staff in Washington, D.C.

In 1914, shortly after the outbreak of the First World War, Mitchell was sent to Europe as an observer. There, he became convinced of the importance of air power to military operations. After earning his wings in 1916 he was placed in charge of the fledgling U.S. Army Air Service, which was administered by the Signal Corps. When the United States entered the Great War in 1917 Mitchell, by then a major, was assigned to General Pershing's staff as head of the American Expeditionary Force's Air Service. In little more than a year he had built the American air arm from a small, untrained detachment with no planes to one of the finest air forces in the world, earning promotion to brigadier general in the process. By the war's end he was slated to command the entire Allied air effort.

On his return to the United States in 1919 General Mitchell was named Assistant Chief of the U.S. Air Service. He quickly became the country's leading spokesman for the importance of air power, continuing an unceasing campaign for a large, independent air force despite opposition from an apathetic Congress and the shortsighted high commands of the army and navy. When his planes clearly demonstrated the importance of air power to modern war-

fare in 1921 by bombing and sinking three obsolete American and German battleships—the first time this had ever been done—Mitchell's superiors felt publicly embarrassed and ordered the general on fact-finding tours to Europe and the Far East to get him out of the public eye.

On his return to the United States in 1924 Mitchell embarked on a new campaign warning Americans of the poor state of U.S. military preparedness, particularly against Japan, which he saw as a major threat to peace in the Pacific. As a result he was removed from his Army Air Service post and demoted to colonel. When he made further public statements regarding incompetence in the War and Navy Departments Colonel Mitchell was court-martialed in December 1925. Found guilty after a sensational trial which succeeded in publicizing his views, Mitchell resigned from the army on February 1, 1926.

Billy Mitchell spent his remaining years as an advocate for American air power. He died in New York on February 19, 1936. Vindicated by the Japanese attack on Pearl Harbor a few years later, Mitchell was posthumously awarded a special Medal of Honor in 1946. A year later his dream of an independent aeronautics branch was realized with the creation of the U.S. Air Force.

IN HIS MORE THAN 50 years of service to the Crown, Admiral Lord Keyes had the most varied and distinguished career of any Royal Navy officer of this century. An indefatigable fighter, he masterminded the most daring naval raid of the First World War and 20 years later came out of retirement to organize the elite combat group that set the standard for covert units the world over—the British Commandos.

Roger John Brownlow Keyes was born in Tundiani, India, on October 4, 1872, the son of General Sir Charles Keyes. He began his naval career as a cadet on board H.M.S. *Brittania* in 1885 and by 1900 had risen to the rank of commander in recognition of his services during China's Boxer Rebellion. In 1910 he was appointed captain in the submarine service, rising within two years to commodore of the entire British submarine fleet.

During the first months of the Great War Commodore Keyes directed English submarine operations in the North Sea, playing a major role in the British victory at the Battle of Heligoland Bight on August 28, 1914. Following this engagement, he was detailed as naval chief of staff to the Gallipoli campaign off of Turkey, receiving a knighthood in 1915 for his services in this ill-fated venture. Upgraded to rear admiral, he spent the next two years in command of a battleship squadron in the North Sea.

In October 1917 Admiral Keyes was appointed director of planning for the British Admiralty. He quickly proved his aptitude for high command by developing a complex plan for sealing off the key German submarine bases at Zeebrugge and Ostend, Belgium. Promoted to vice admiral, he personally executed the operation on April 23, 1917. In a combined land–sea attack foreshadowing the commando raids of later wars Keyes successfully neutralized the shore batteries guarding the ports, blocked access routes for German reinforcements, and sank several outdated cruisers in the approach channels to

prevent the U-boats from leaving port. The raid marked Keyes as one of Britain's finest naval commanders, and he finished the war a national hero.

In the years following the Great War, Sir Roger served as deputy chief of staff at the Admiralty and as commander of the Mediterranean fleet, winning promotion to admiral of the fleet in May 1930. He retired from the Royal Navy in 1935 but returned to active duty during the Second World War at the request of Prime

Minister Winston Churchill, who asked him to establish an elite mobile strike force in June 1940. In less than a year he had organized and trained the first British Commando battalion, and in October 1941, with his job complete, he was relieved of duty. Two years later Admiral Keyes was elevated to baron in recognition of his long-standing service to the Crown. Lord Keyes died at Buckingham, England, on December 26, 1945.

Adm. Roger Keyes, an outstanding English naval hero of both World Wars and the creator of the famed British commandos, as he appeared at the end of the Great War.

ANTHONY McAULIFFE

United States, 1898–1975

SOME GENERALS HAVE risen to fame through their leadership on the battlefield; others, by their brilliance at strategic planning. Gen. Anthony McAuliffe achieved immortality during the Battle of the Bulge by his unequivocal, one-word response to a German demand for surrender—"Nuts!"

Anthony Clement McAuliffe was born in Washington, D.C., on July 2, 1898, the grandson of Irish immigrants. Raised in the capital area, he attended the University of West Virginia for one year before being admitted to the U.S. Military Academy in 1917. The First World War caused McAuliffe's class to be rushed through West Point, and he graduated in the fall of 1918 as a lieutenant of field artillery. The Armistice was declared before he could embark for France, however, so he resumed his studies until the following June. Assigned to posts throughout the United States, the promising young officer was promoted to captain in 1935 and appointed to the Army Command School the following year.

With the outbreak of the Second World War in 1939 Captain McAuliffe was sent to the Army War College for additional training. Upon his graduation he was promoted to major and assigned to weapons development, rising to the rank of colonel by February 1942. In August of that year McAuliffe was named artillery commander of Gen. Maxwell Taylor's 101st Airborne Division and promoted to brigadier general. Although he had earlier suffered a broken back in training, he parachuted to Normandy with the division on the night before D-Day and was named the unit's second-in-command when his predecessor was killed in action. He subsequently led his troops in airborne assaults into the Netherlands and northern France.

When Field Marshal Gerd von Rundstedt's Germans launched their counterattack against the Allied invasion in the Ardennes on December 16, 1944—known as the Battle of the Bulge—the 101st Division was in Rheims, France. General McAuliffe, who was in acting command of the "Screaming Eagles"—as the unit was known—rushed his men overland to hold the strategic crossroads village of Bastogne. Rapidly surrounded by the Nazi advance, he was invited by the Germans to surrender on December 22. Instead he issued his

Gen. Anthony McAuliffe, the unflappable commander of the U.S. 101 Airborne Division during the Battle of the Bulge.

famous refusal and, although his troops were outnumbered four to one, he held the position until he was relieved by Gen. George S. Patton's forces on the 26th. In recognition of his heroism, General Patton personally awarded McAuliffe the Distinguished Service Cross, the army's second highest combat award.

McAuliffe was subsequently promoted to major general and assigned command of the 103rd Infantry Division,

which he led through Alsace to the Alps, capturing Innsbruck and the strategic Brenner Pass in late April 1945. After the war he supervised the atomic tests on Bikini Atoll in 1946 and was appointed head of the Army Chemical Corps three years later. General McAuliffe retired from the army in 1956 and died in Washington, D.C., on August 11, 1975.

FIELD MARSHAL
KEMAL ATATÜRK
Turkey, 1881–1938

KEMAL ATATÜRK TOWERS as the central figure of modern Turkish history. The first president of Turkey and the man who created a modern nation out of the ruins of the Ottoman Empire, Atatürk was also his country's greatest military leader in the early years of the 20th century.

Atatürk was born to Turkish parents in Salonika, Greece (then part of the Ottoman Empire) in 1881; the exact date is unknown, although in later life he claimed May 19 as his birthday. As a boy he was dubbed Mustafa Kemal—Turkish for perfection—because of the high standards he set for himself and for others.

The future general graduated from the military academy at Monastir in 1899. After attending the army staff college in Constantinople, he was commissioned a lieutenant and posted to Syria as punishment for his radical views about political reform. The move failed to dampen his spirits, however, and he proceeded to organize a secret society within the army dedicated to improving conditions in Turkey. Despite concerns over Atatürk's political opinions, he was recognized as an outstanding officer and by 1907 he had risen to the rank of major.

Mustafa Kemal first distinguished himself in combat in 1911 during the Italo-Turkish War for control of Libya. In one of the few successful Turkish campaigns of that struggle, the young major kept the Italian forces near Cyrenaica pinned to the seacoast, thus preventing them from further offensive actions. Promoted to colonel, Kemal subsequently served as a staff officer during the Balkan Wars in 1912/13 and as Turkish military attache to Bulgaria.

When the Ottoman Empire entered the First World War on the side of the Central Powers in October 1914, Colonel Kemal was placed in command of the Turkish Army's 19th Division guarding the Gallipoli Peninsula to the north of the Dardanelles. His determined defense of this strategically important peninsula against a British invasion in April 1915 kept the assaulting forces trapped on three narrow beacheads for eight months until they gave up their plans and withdrew. Kemal became a national hero and was promoted to general. He finished the war as commander in Syria, where he held together the army during its final retreat from Damascus.

Following the Turkish surrender on October 30, 1918, the 600-year-old Ottoman Empire rapidly crumbled. An attempted Greek invasion in 1921 was driven back by General Kemal, greatly increasing his popularity among the Turks. He was promoted to field marshal in 1922 and elected Turkey's first president when the sultan was deposed the following year. Assuming the name Kemal Atatürk—"father of the Turks"—he ruled his country as a benevolent dictator, bringing about the Westernizing reforms he had dreamed of for 20 years. Kemal Atatürk died in office in Istanbul on November 10, 1938.

Kemal Atatürk, the father of modern Turkey whose dogged defense of Gallipoli dealt the Allies their worst defeat in World War I.

GERD VON RUNDSTEDT

Germany, 1875–1953

FIELD MARSHAL Gerd von Runstedt was one of the finest field commanders of the Second World War. His outstanding leadership led to several of the Third Reich's most important victories and enabled him to advance to the highest levels of command despite his lack of ardor for the Nazi Party.

Von Rundstedt was born in Aschersleben, Germany, on December 12, 1875. Commissioned an officer in the Prussian infantry in 1893 he advanced rapidly, serving on the German general staffs in Turkey and France during the First World War. During the 1920s he rose to national prominence, earning promotion to major general in 1927 and lieutenant general in 1929. In October 1938 he was assigned to oversee the German occupation of the Sudetenland (a portion of Czechoslovakia annexed by Hitler in that year), after which he retired from the Wehrmacht with the rank of full general.

At the onset of the Second World War in September 1939 the 63-year-old von Rundstedt returned to duty. Placed in charge of one of the two army groups that invaded Poland in the wake of Heinz Guderian's Panzer divisions, von Rundstedt played a key role in the Blitzkrieg campaign, trapping the southern Polish army before it could retreat to Warsaw. The following spring he commanded the Third Reich's invasion of France, earning promotion to field marshal for his success.

Field Marshal von Rundstedt scored his greatest victory during the Nazi advance into Russia in 1941. Assigned command of the German forces attacking the Ukraine, he secured the entire area within three months, inflicting incredible losses on the Russian army in the process. At Kiev alone, on September 26, he succeeded in capturing 665,000 of Stalin's soldiers, the largest single surrender in history.

As winter approached, Marshal von Rundstedt, like General Guderian, had serious misgivings about Hitler's direction of the Russian campaign. After retreating from an untenable position at Rostov he was relieved of his command on December 1. Within four months however, the mercurial Fuehrer recalled the field marshal, naming him commander in chief of the German forces in Western Europe. After failing to stop the Allies' D-Day invasion of Normandy

in June 1944 and unable to fulfill the Fuehrer's unrealistic expectations for the Battle of the Bulge that winter, Field Marshall von Rundstedt was again dismissed by Hitler in March 1945. The 70-year-old field marshal was subsequently captured by the British and briefly detained on suspicion of war crimes, but he was released due to ill health. Field Marshal Gerd von Rundstedt died in Hannover, Germany, on February 23, 1953.

Field Marshal Gerd von Rundstedt, the brilliant tactician who in this photo looks very much like Hollywood's quintessential Nazi general.

JAMES DOOLITTLE

United States, 1896–

IN THE WAKE OF THE Japanese bombing of Pearl Harbor on December 7, 1941, the United States forces in the Pacific faced bleak months of defeat and retreat. Then in April 1942 American morale was given a badly needed boost when U.S. Army Air Force bombers retaliated against Japan in a stunning surprise attack of their own. The daring raid was led by a flier already recognized as one of the greatest pilots in aviation history—"Jimmy" Doolittle.

James Harold Doolittle was born on December 14, 1896, in Alameda, California, and raised in Los Angeles and Nome, Alaska, where his father went

prospecting for gold. When the United States entered the First World War Doolittle left the University of California to enlist in the Army Air Service. He won his wings on March 11, 1918, and was assigned as a flying instructor in the states.

In the years after the war Lieutenant Doolittle became nationally famous for a series of spectacular test flights that he made for the army and navy. He became the first pilot, for example, to fly coast-to-coast in less than 24 hours and the first to demonstrate the efficacy of flying "blind." By 1930, when he resigned from active duty due to his "advanced age" for a pilot (he was all of 34), he had risen to the rank of major,

won two Distinguished Flying Crosses, and earned a Doctor of Science degree in aeronautical engineering from the Massachusetts Institute of Technology.

For ten years Doolittle worked in private industry, until the prospect of war led to his recall to duty on July 1, 1940. He helped develop army mobilization plans until January 1942, when he was promoted to lieutenant colonel and assigned to organize a bombing raid on Japan. After determining that B-25 long-range bombers could indeed take off from an aircraft carrier—something that had never been attempted before—he supervised every aspect of the mission from training the men to modifying the

equipment. On April 18, 1942, he led his task force of 16 B-25s on their 600-mile flight to Japan. Reaching Tokyo at mid-day, the raiders bombed several defense plants without any losses to themselves and then flew on to China, where they were forced to ditch their planes due to a lack of fuel. Two crews were subsequently captured by the Japanese. The mission was considered a spectacular success, winning Doolittle the Congressional Medal of Honor and the stars of a brigadier general.

In November 1942, General Doolittle served as commander of the 12th Air Force during the invasion of North Africa. Promoted to major general, he was subsequently appointed head of the 15th Air Force in Italy in 1943 and then the Eighth Air Force in England in 1944. After V-E Day he was transferred with his unit to the Pacific theater and ended the war on Okinawa as a lieutenant general.

After the war General Doolittle returned to his business career, serving as the director of several prominent corporations and as a member of numerous government advisory boards. Retired, he now lives in Santa Monica, California.

(Right) The inimitable Jimmy Doolittle, already one of the greatest aviators in history before his famous raid on Tokyo in 1942.

(Opposite) Doolittle and some of the bombing mission crewmen who made it safely to China after the raid. From the left: Sgt. F. A. Braemer; Sgt. P. J. Leonard; Lt. R. E. Cole; Doolittle; and Lieutenant Potter.

AT THE BEGINNING OF the Great War the immense German sea force created by Admiral von Tirpitz posed the greatest threat to the British navy since Nelson met the French at Trafalgar. This time the awesome responsibility for safeguarding the Grand Fleet—and with it, Britain's independence—fell to Adm. John Jellicoe, who commanded one of the largest naval actions in history, the Battle of Jutland.

John Rushworth Jellicoe was born in Southampton, England, on December 5, 1859, the son of a merchant seaman. Young Jellicoe began his service in the Royal Navy as a 12-year-old cadet in 1872. Within five years he was commanding a British squadron in the Russo-Turkish War. In 1878 he was appointed to the Royal Naval College at Greenwich, from which he graduated with honors. During his subsequent tours of duty Lieutenant Jellicoe became an expert on naval ordnance, and in 1889 was assigned to the Admiralty to assist with the rearmament of the British fleet, earning a promotion to commander. By 1910 he had risen to vice admiral in charge of the Atlantic fleet, and two years later was appointed second lord of the admiralty.

At the outbreak of the First World War in August 1914 Jellicoe was promoted to full admiral and placed in command of the Grand Fleet, Britain's main sea force in the North Atlantic. The Germans avoided any major confrontations with Jellicoe's ships until the end of May 1916, when the Kaiser's forces under Adm. Reinhard Scheer moved into the North Sea hoping to lure the British into combat. Admiral Jellicoe had anticipated Scheer's movement, however, and on May 31 he decoyed the German fleet into battle in waters of his own choosing off the coast of Jutland. Jellicoe's 150 battleships and cruisers sparred with Scheer's armada of 101 vessels across a vast expanse of the North Sea (the scale of the battle prevented all but a small percentage of each fleet from active engagement at one time, so the Russo-Japanese Battle of Tsushima remains the century's most intensive naval battle). After exchanging fire with Jellicoe's warships throughout the afternoon and most of the night Scheer ordered his badly damaged fleet to return to port. Having lost a battleship, five cruisers, and five destroyers, he did not risk another

The stalwart Adm. Sir John Jellicoe, savior of the British grand fleet in the World War I Battle of Jutland.

general engagement for the rest of the war. Although Admiral Jellicoe failed to destroy the German navy as he had hoped, he succeeded in securing for Britain the strategically vital control of the North Sea. More importantly, as Winston Churchill pointed out, Jellicoe avoided the mistakes that could have lost Britain the war in a single day.

In November Sir John, a national hero, was reappointed to the Admiralty as First Sea Lord, from which he organized Britain's convoy system of defense against German U-boat attacks on the high seas. Although he was ousted in a purely political move at the end of 1917 he remained one of Britain's most highly respected naval commanders, becoming a viscount in January 1918, admiral of the fleet the following year, and later an earl. In 1920 Lord Jellicoe was appointed governor-general of New Zealand, where he served until 1924, when he retired from active duty. Admiral Jellicoe died at his home in London, on November 20, 1935, and is buried in a place of honor next to Admiral Nelson in St. Paul's Cathedral.

MARESUKE NOGI
Japan, 1849–1912

FOR GENERATIONS, adherence to the samurai code of *bushido*—total dedication to duty, country, and emperor—has been the highest aspiration of the Japanese soldier. The individual who most closely embodied *bushido* in modern times was the man hailed as "the incarnation of the Imperial war god," the commander of the victorious Japanese army in the Russo-Japanese War, Gen. Lord Maresuke Nogi.

Maresuke Nogi was born in Tokyo in 1849. His father, a provincial government official and dedicated nationalist, imbued Maresuke with his strong commitment to public service. In 1871, after the Meiji Restoration and the establishment of the Imperial Japanese Army, the 22-year-old Maresuke enlisted, seeing a military career as a perfect opportunity to serve the emperor. Commissioned a major, the talented officer rose to command of the 14th Regiment within two years.

During the Satsuma Rebellion of 1877 an event occurred which profoundly affected Nogi for the rest of his life. At the Battle of Kagoshima his regiment lost its colors to the enemy, a disgrace for which the Japanese code of honor demanded *seppuku*, or ritual suicide, by the unit's commander. The Meiji Emperor recognized that Colonel Nogi was not at fault and excused him from committing *hara-kiri*; thereafter, Nogi felt that he owed his life to the emperor and dedicated himself entirely to Imperial service. Remaining in the army, he was promoted to brigadier general in 1878, rising to major general seven years later.

General Nogi first achieved international prominence during the Sino-Japanese War in 1894 when he captured the 10,000-man garrison at Port Arthur, China, with the loss of only 18 Japanese soldiers. Nogi was rewarded with elevation to baron and promotion to lieutenant general, but his victory was hollow; under foreign diplomatic pressure the Japanese abandoned the base only to have the Russians seize Port Arthur after they left, thus sowing seeds of dissension which erupted into a war between Japan and Russia ten years later.

When the Japanese high command moved to recapture Port Arthur in 1904, knowing it would lead to war, they planned a combined operation between the naval forces of Adm. Heihachiro

Togo and the Third Army under Lord Nogi, then a full general. While Togo's ships kept the Russian fleet trapped in the harbor, General Nogi was responsible for capturing the heavily manned fortifications on the hills ringing the city. After a four-month campaign which cost more than 59,000 Japanese casualties—including Nogi's two sons—the general's troops succeeded on December 5 in securing the key Russian stronghold on towering 203 Meter Hill. Thereafter the Japanese artillery was able to force the Russian garrison into surrender within a matter of days, on January 1, 1905. Lord Nogi followed his victory at Port Arthur by driving the Russians from Manchuria that March in the final land campaign of the war, the Battle of Mukden.

Nogi returned to Japan a hero. The Meiji Emperor made him a count and appointed him to supervise the education of Prince Hirohito, his grandson. When the emperor died in 1912, General Nogi felt that his old debt of honor to the sovereign required him to join his ruler in death. On the evening of the emperor's funeral, September 13, 1912, Lord Nogi and his wife committed *seppuku* at their home in Tokyo. The building has been preserved as a shrine to the memory of this outstanding general.

Lord Maresuke Nogi, the outstanding turn-of-the-century Japanese general who has been described as the last Samurai.

OMAR BRADLEY

United States, 1893–1981

OMAR BRADLEY WAS ONE of the most widely respected American commanders of the Second World War. A thoroughly professional soldier, his meticulous planning and obvious care

(Opposite) Omar Bradley, last of America's five-star generals. Soft-spoken and thoroughly professional, he was one of the most popular American commanders of World War II.

(Below) General Bradley (center) at the Normandy beachhead with Adms. Alan Kirk, Jr., (left) and John Hall. An active front-line commander, Bradley was one of the first American generals to land at Omaha Beach.

for his men earned him the nickname "the G.I.'s general."

Omar Nelson Bradley was born in Clark, Missouri, on February 12, 1893. His father died when he was 13, and Omar, like many other good students of limited means, applied to the U.S. Military Academy for an education. He graduated from West Point in 1915, as did his friend Dwight Eisenhower, and was commissioned a lieutenant of infantry.

After brief service on the Mexican border Lieutenant Bradley was detailed to a base in Washington state, where he remained through most of the First World War, much to his disappointment.

He subsequently served as a mathematics and tactics instructor at West Point and as a training officer at Fort Benning, Georgia, where he greatly impressed the assistant commandant, Lt. Col. George C. Marshall. In 1940, when the U.S. Army began its buildup in preparation for war, Marshall, then Chief of Staff, appointed Bradley commandant of the fort with the rank of brigadier general. Bradley proceeded to organize a model program capable of training 14,000 officers at a time. When the United States entered the war in December 1941 he was promoted to major general and assigned to mobilize the famed 82nd and 28th Divisions in Louisiana.

General Bradley received his first field command in February 1943. When the Allied offensive in North Africa stalled that month, Marshall appointed him deputy commander of the Second Corps in Tunisia, where he acted as a troubleshooter for Commanding General Eisenhower. His precise analysis of the situation on that front and his capture of Bizerta in May brought him promotion to lieutenant general and command of the corps after his predecessor, George S. Patton, was made head of the Seventh Army.

Bradley led the Second Corps with distinction through the invasion of Sicily that summer. At the campaign's conclusion in September he was transferred to England to mobilize the U.S. First Army for the Normandy invasion the following spring. Bradley, who came ashore on Omaha beach within 30 hours of the first D-Day landings on June 6, 1944, played a decisive role in coordinating the assault and directing the American advance through the German lines to the south. Subsequently given command of the 1.3 million soldiers of the 12th Army Group—comprising all the U.S. troops in northern France—he supervised the final American advance across the Rhine and into central Germany, a carefully planned campaign that brought him promotion to full general in March 1945.

After the German surrender in May "the G.I.'s general" returned to the United States to head the Veterans Administration. In February 1948 he succeeded Eisenhower as Army Chief of Staff, and in August 1949 was appointed Chairman of the Joint Chiefs of Staff, with promotion to general of the army the following year. General Bradley stepped down from active duty in 1953 and died in New York on April 8, 1981, the last of America's five-star generals.

Bradley reviewing his troops in Germany shortly before the end of the war in Europe. His concern for the common soldier earned him the nickname, "the G.I.'s General."

RAV ALUF
MOSHE DAYAN
Israel, 1915–1981

FOR 25 YEARS, Moshe Dayan served as Israel's top military commander. A leader in the 1948 War for Independence, he subsequently distinguished himself with stunning victories in the Suez Conflict of 1956 and the Six-Day War of 1967.

Moshe Dayan was born on May 4, 1915, in Deganiah, Palestine, the first child born in Israel's first kibbutz. At the age of 14 he joined the Haganah. It was with this Jewish underground organization that he first demonstrated his natural talents as a military commander, distinguishing himself in retaliatory raids against the Arabs in the 1930s. The British, who ruled Palestine at that time, arrested Dayan for his activities in 1939 but released him from prison in 1941 to organize a company of commandos to fight the Vichy forces in Syria. While leading an assault against these French collaborators on June 8 he received a bad face wound which cost him his left eye and earned him his trademark black eye patch.

At the close of the Second World War Dayan again joined the Haganah, rising to the rank of major by the time of the Israeli War for Independence in May 1948. His defense of the crucial Jordan Valley established him as one of the Israeli's best officers and earned him command of the Jerusalem front as successor to David "Mickey" Marcus that August. Despite heavy Arab attacks Dayan held the line in the Holy City until the end of the war on July 20, 1949, and in reward was promoted to *rav aluf* (major general) in November.

In 1953, Dayan was named Israeli Army Chief of Staff, and three years later led his forces in their unprecedented sweep through Gaza and the Sinai during the Suez War with Egypt. He retired from the army in 1958 to enter politics, and after serving several years as minister of agriculture was appointed minister of defense on June 1, 1967. In the Six-Day War, which ensued on June 5–10, he directed the Israeli army in a repeat of its 1956 rout of the Egyptian armed forces in the Sinai, mounting one

of the most effective surprise attacks in modern history.

Dayan remained as minister of defense until the 1973 Yom Kippur War with Egypt. When Israel was caught unprepared by the Egyptian attack on October 6, he was severely criticized for the army's early losses in the Sinai despite the fact that he quickly brought up reinforcements which regained the lost territory. Dismissed in March 1974, he was appointed foreign minister by Prime Minister Menachem Begin four years later. In that capacity he played a key role in negotiating the Camp David Accords and the Israeli-Egyptian Peace Treaty in 1979. He retired from public service shortly thereafter and died in Tel Aviv, Israel, on October 16, 1981.

(Opposite) Moshe Dayan during a tour of Israel's defenses on the border with Jordan in 1969.

(Below) Dayan surveying the Israeli positions north of the GolanHeights during the Yom Kippur War of 1973.

THE ALLIED CAMPAIGN IN China and Burma was one of the longest and most difficult operations of the Second World War. Its success was largely due to the tactical skill and inspiring leadership of the commander of the Sino-American forces in the Far East during the first years of the war, the acerbic, no-nonsense Gen. "Vinegar Joe" Stilwell.

Joseph Warren Stilwell was born in Palatka, Florida, on March 19, 1883, and raised in Yonkers, New York. He applied for admission to the U.S. Military Academy because his father decided that he needed more discipline than he would get at Yale. Following his graduation from West Point in 1904 the young lieutenant, who was an expert linguist, was detailed to the Philippines and later recalled to the Military Academy as a language instructor. During the First World War he served in staff positions in France, rising to the rank of colonel, and winning the Distinguished Service Medal for his part in directing the St. Mihiel offensive in 1918.

Shortly after the end of the war he became American military attaché in Peking. He spent most of the next 20 years in China as an army observer and commander, learning to speak several Chinese dialects fluently. He returned to the United States only once between 1919 and 1939, for advanced infantry training at Fort Benning, Georgia, where his moody disposition earned him the nickname "Vinegar Joe." He was recalled to the United States in 1939, promoted to brigadier general, and placed in charge of the Third Infantry Brigade. Later he was given command of the newly organized Seventh Division as a major general.

In February 1942, after the United States' entry into the Second World War, Stilwell was upgraded to lieutenant general, appointed head of all American forces in China, Burma, and India and, at the request of Chiang Kai-shek, named the Generalissimo's chief of staff commanding the Chinese Fifth and Sixth Armies as well. Assigned that May to defend eastern Burma from Japanese invasion, he received "a hell of a beating," as he put it, and was forced to retreat into India. Returning to China, he spent most of the following year training his Chinese troops and harassing the Japanese on the ground while Claire Chennault's 14th Air Force

attacked them from above. By the beginning of 1944 Stilwell's American and Chinese troops were ready to move against the Japanese in Burma, and after a difficult nine-month campaign succeeded in recapturing the northern part of the country, reopening vital land and rail routes to China.

Although an excellent tactician and inspiring leader, "Vinegar Joe" was no diplomat. He did not get along with General Chennault or the British, and he treated Chiang Kai-shek with barely concealed contempt, calling him "Peanut Head" in his diary. Finally in

October 1944 Chiang had him removed from China. Stilwell, by that point a full general, ended the war as U.S. commander at Okinawa. After his return to the United States in September 1945 he was put in charge of the army installations on the Pacific Coast. He died in San Francisco, California, on October 12, 1946.

"Vinegar Joe" Stilwell sporting his famous cigarette holder, a trademark that became almost as familiar during the war as Douglas MacArthur's oversized corncob pipe.

Stilwell in Burma
during the Allied
counteroffensive
of 1944. The
general won the
respect of his
command by
sharing in the
hardships of
jungle living for
weeks at a time.

ERWIN ROMMEL

Germany, 1891–1944

BY ITS VERY NATURE the repressive Nazi regime of Adolf Hitler produced few popular military heroes. An exception to this was the colorful leader of Germany's Afrikakorps, the legendary "Desert Fox," Field Marshal Erwin Rommel.

Erwin Rommel was born in Heidenheim, Germany, on November 15, 1891. In 1910, he entered the German army as a cadet in the 124th Infantry, earning a lieutenant's commission two years later. During the First World War he served as an infantry officer in Italy and France, winning both the Iron Cross and the Pour le Mérite.

Rommel remained in the infantry after the war, becoming a highly respected instructor of tactics and rising to the rank of colonel. In 1938 his selection as

(Opposite) The face of the Desert Fox—Field Marshal Erwin Rommel.

(Below) Rommel in the North African desert, where he earned his reputation as a superb field commander. The general is partaking of a commodity even more important to his campaign than fuel or ammunition—fresh water.

head of Adolf Hitler's bodyguard placed him within the Fuehrer's inner circle.

It was not until 1940 that Rommel was appointed to the tank command that would make him famous. Assigned to lead the Seventh Panzer Division in the offensive against France, he spearheaded the German attack at Dinant on May 12, bridging the Meuse River and destroying the French Ninth Army in just three days. The victory marked Rommel as one of the Third Reich's finest Panzer leaders and in February 1941 earned him command of the famed Afrikakorps with the rank of lieutenant general.

The "Desert Fox" amassed an impressive string of victories in his first months of fighting in the North African campaign. By June he had driven the British out of Libya and well into Egypt, for which he was promoted to field marshal. Six months later, he maintained control over the area by successfully fending off a counteroffensive despite a shortage of fuel for his tanks, but the arrival of Britain's Gen. (later Field Marshal) Bernard L. Montgomery in August proved too much for him to handle. Outmaneuvered by Montgomery in the

extended Battle of El Alamein that fall, the "Desert Fox" was driven out of Libya into Tunisia, where he was decisively defeated at the Battle of Medenine on March 5, 1943.

Rommel's loss at Medenine did not shake Hitler's faith in the field marshal's abilities. He was named personal adviser to the Fuehrer and was later assigned the command of an army group in Italy. In January 1944 he was appointed head of the German forces defending northern France under Field Marshal Gerd von Rundstedt. In this capacity, he prepared careful plans for repulsing the anticipated Allied invasion in a strongly fortified coastal zone, but von Rundstedt dismissed his strategy with disastrous results for the Third Reich that June.

Field Marshal Rommel was subsequently linked with the July 1944 officers' plot to assassinate Hitler. Given the choice between summary execution by the S.S. and committing suicide, he chose the latter. Erwin Rommel died in Herrlingen, Germany, on October 14, 1944.

Field Marshal Rommel surveying German defenses along the Atlantic coast of France a few months before the Allied invasion. He proposed detailed plans for repulsing such an attack but was ignored by the Nazi high command.

GENERAL
SIR REDVERS BULLER
United Kingdom, 1839–1908

THE TURN OF THE 20TH CENTURY saw the British army engaged in a protracted war with Dutch Boers over control of the riches of South Africa. The leader of the forces that emerged triumphant in this war was Gen. Sir Redvers Buller, one of England's finest field commanders at the close of the Victorian era.

Redvers Buller was born at Downes, England, on December 7, 1839, the scion of one of the area's oldest landed families. A graduate of Eton, he began his career in the army in 1858 when he was commissioned an ensign (sublieutenant) in the King's Royal Rifles. Buller spent the next 28 years at posts in India, Canada, and Africa, receiving a knighthood for his part in the Egyptian campaign of 1882. Sir Redvers subsequently served with distinction as chief of staff during the Sudan uprising of 1884 and as adjutant general of the British army, rising to the rank of full general on June 24, 1896.

At the outbreak of the Boer War in October 1899 General Buller, by virtue of his seniority and previous experience, was selected to command a force of 70,000 men charged with protecting British interests against the Boers in South Africa. Buller was clearly more effective as a field commander than an overall strategist, and he was soon replaced as commander in chief by Field Marshal Lord Roberts, a move that enabled him to take his proper place at the head of his troops. His first triumph occurred at the relief of Ladysmith, a British stronghold that had been surrounded by Boers under the command of Louis Botha. After a campaign of two months, General Buller's forces succeeded in driving Botha's Afrikaners from Ladysmith on February 28, 1900, setting the stage for a British offensive into the Afrikaner's homeland, the Transvaal. Buller pressed the Boers northward, finally trapping Botha's forces near Belfast. General Buller's decisive victory over Botha at the Battle of Bergendal on August 27 crippled the Boer army and effectively ended the Afrikaners' struggle for independence.

When Sir Redvers Buller returned to England in November he was awarded the Grand Cross of the Order of Saint Michael and Saint George and given command of the First Army Corps. Buller's military career ended in October 1901 when he was removed from his post for making a politically damaging speech. The general died at his country home in Crediton, England, on June 2, 1908.

Sir Redvers Buller wearing the kind of ornate uniform that typified the British Empire during the Victorian Age.

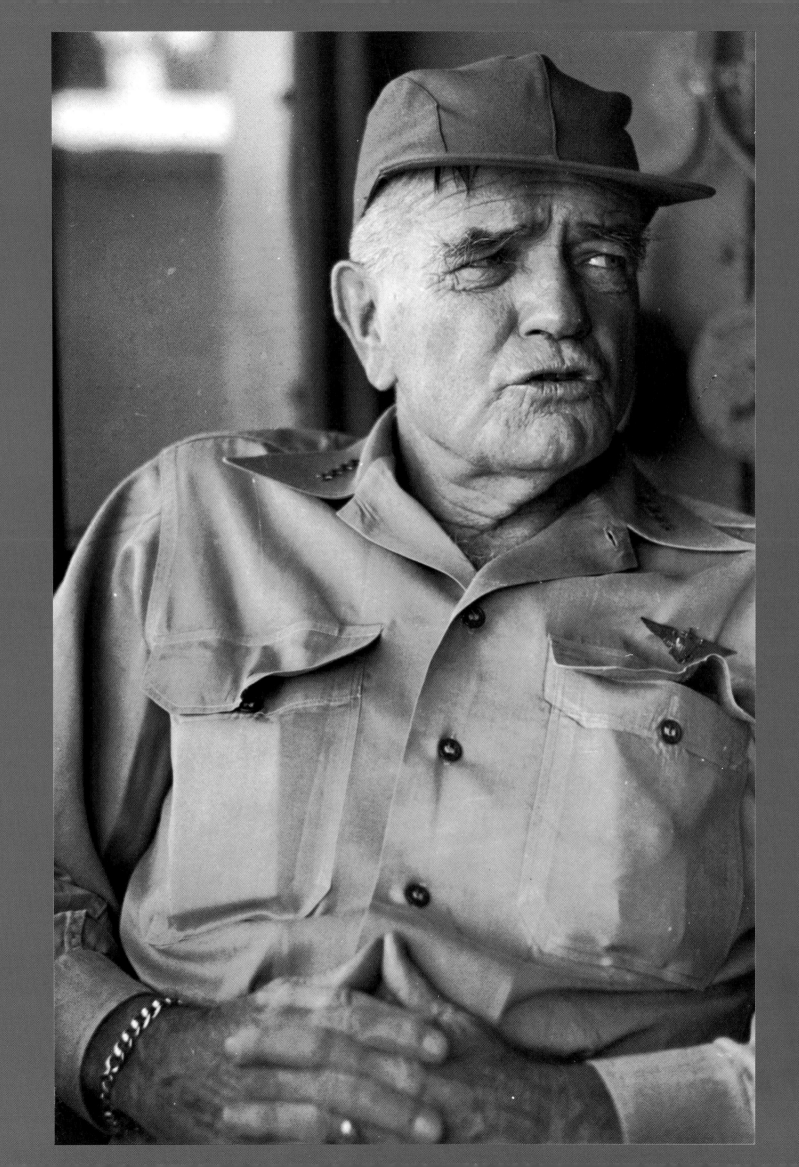

WILLIAM HALSEY

United States, 1882–1959

IN THE MONTHS AFTER the attack on Pearl Harbor, Adm. William Halsey emerged as one of America's finest naval commanders. Not only was he the nation's top carrier strategist, he was also a charismatic leader whose unwavering determination inspired his men to victory and earned him the popular sobriquet "Bull."

William Frederick Halsey, Jr. was born in Elizabeth, New Jersey, on October 30, 1882. The son of a navy captain, he entered the U.S. Naval Academy in 1900 and, in the custom of the day, was commissioned an ensign two years after his graduation in 1904. He subsequently served in the Vera Cruz expedition in 1914 and in antisubmarine service during the First World War, rising to the rank of commander. In the late 1920s he developed his interest in the navy's fledgling carrier service, and in 1935, after several years of training, he was given command of the carrier *Saratoga*. Promoted to rear admiral three years later, he was appointed head of a carrier division in the Pacific, rising to vice admiral in charge of the Pacific Aircraft Battle Force in 1940.

When the Japanese attacked Pearl Harbor on December 7, 1941, Halsey's carrier fleet was at sea and escaped unharmed. Under the direction of Adm. Chester Nimitz, he led the surviving armada in the navy's first counterstrike against the Japanese on the Marshall Islands in February, greatly boosting American morale. Two months later he commanded the carrier force that launched Jimmy Doolittle's raid on Tokyo.

Although he was on medical leave during the Battle of Midway in May 1942, Halsey returned to duty, taking command of the Guadalcanal campaign in August, winning that strategic island in November, and earning promotion to full admiral. By early 1944 his Third Fleet had secured the entire South Pacific for the Allies, and in October had decisively driven the Japanese navy from the Philippines while supporting Gen. Douglas MacArthur's invasion. After this victory, he turned his attention to the campaign for Okinawa, which was captured in June 1945. He ended the war as commander of the U.S. forces off of Japan. The Japanese surrender was signed on his flagship, the U.S.S. *Missouri*, on September 2.

In recognition of his outstanding leadership Halsey was promoted to fleet admiral in December 1945. He retired from active duty two years later, and died at Fisher's Island, New York, on August 16, 1959.

(Opposite) This candid photo of Adm. William Halsey captures the determination that earned him the popular nickname, "Bull."

(Below) Halsey aboard his flagship. Unlike the Pacific theater commander Admiral Nimitz, who was tied to an office for most of the war, Halsey was almost constantly on duty at sea directing fleet operations.

SIR JOHN MONASH

Australia, 1865–1931

THE FIRST WORLD WAR was truly an international struggle, involving soldiers from every corner of the globe. Some of the best troops among the Allied forces were the Anzacs—the Australian and New Zealand Army Corps—and one of the best commanders was their leader at the close of the war, Sir John Monash.

Monash was born to German Jewish parents in Melbourne, Australia, on June 27, 1865. Although he trained as an engineer and a lawyer, he had a keen interest in the military and enlisted in the Australian militia as an artillery lieutenant in 1887. His enthusiasm and skill earned him steady promotions, and after a stint in the Intelligence Corps he was commissioned a colonel of infantry in 1913.

At the onset of the Great War in 1914 Colonel Monash was called to active duty and given command of Australia's Fourth Infantry Brigade. Along with the rest of the Anzac troops, he received his baptism of fire during the disastrous Gallipoli campaign against Turkey the following spring. In this offensive, which began on April 25, 1915, some 78,000 Allied troops made a fruitless attempt to capture the strategic Gallipoli peninsula that overlooks the Dardanelles. The Anzacs made several gallant attempts to storm the high grounds dominating their narrow beachhead, but each time they were beaten back with heavy losses by Col. Mustafa Kemal's Turkish forces.

After an eight-month stalemate, the Allied troops were finally withdrawn in December. Monash, by then a brigadier general, was assigned to France with the rest of the Anzacs. Promoted to major general in June 1916, he was given command of a new division which he led with distinction at the Battle of Messines and the Third Battle of Ypres in 1917. In recognition of his accomplishments he was made a Knight Commander of the Bath that December, and in June 1918 was given command of the Anzacs with the rank of lieutenant general.

Sir John's finest hour occurred at the Battle of Hamel on July 4. There, he directed a coordinated assault by his Anzacs, the Royal Tank Corps, and the RAF which has been hailed as the first modern battle in history. In the months that followed General Monash spearheaded the Allies' Amiens offensive, breaking through the German lines on August 8 and scoring strategic victories at Péronne and Mont St. Quentin, victories that marked the beginning of the end for the Kaiser's army. Thereafter, Monash and his troops were placed on leave until the Armistice.

At the end of the war Sir John remained in the Australian army, retiring in 1930 with the rank of full general. General Monash died at his home in Melbourne on October 8, 1931.

Australian Gen. Sir John Monash, the hard-hitting leader of the legendary Anzacs in the final days of World War I.

LEADERS OF MEN

MAXIMILIAN, COUNT VON SPEE

MAXIMILIAN, Count von Spee experienced the most dramatic rise and fall of any leader during the First World War. One of the leading naval commanders of the early 20th century, he became a national hero with his stunning defeat of the British navy task force in the eastern Pacific, but a month later his victory was reversed in a battle off the Falklands that destroyed the German navy's Pacific fleet.

Von Spee was born to a noble German family in Copenhagen, Denmark, on June 22, 1861. The young count (*Graf*) entered the Imperial German Navy at the age of 17 in 1878, and by 1910 had risen to the rank of rear admiral. Two years later he was promoted to vice admiral and assigned command of the German fleet in the Pacific, based at Germany's trading port in Tsingtau, China.

At the onset of the First World War in August 1914 von Spee—determined not to be trapped by the mighty Japanese navy as the Russians had been at Port Arthur a few years earlier—set sail with his fleet for the eastern Pacific. From there, he planned to round Cape Horn and harass British shipping in the South Atlantic.

Recognizing this German threat, the British Admiralty dispatched Adm. Sir Christopher Cradock to prevent von Spee from crossing into the Atlantic. Cradock's small force of three cruisers and one armed liner encountered the German's flotilla of five heavy cruisers off the coast of Coronel, Chile, on the evening of November 1, 1914. Within one hour von Spee's highly trained crews and superior firepower had decimated the British squadron, sinking Cradock's flagship and one other cruiser in the English navy's worst defeat in well over a century.

The British responded by sending an armada of eight cruisers and a battleship under Adm. Sir Frederick Sturdee to await von Spee off the Falkland Islands in the South Atlantic. Sturdee's fleet surprised the Germans there on December 8, sinking all but one of von

Vice Adm. Maximillian, Count von Spee, the daring commander who led the Kaiser's Pacific fleet to the greatest German naval victory of World War I.

Spee's ships and causing the loss of 1,800 German sailors, including Admiral von Spee and his two sons.

Left with only von Tirpitz's North Sea fleet, Germany was eliminated as an international sea power by this defeat.

Following his death Maximilian, Count von Spee was hailed as a fallen hero. His memory was honored by the Third Reich with the construction of the pocket battleship *Admiral Graf Spee* in 1934.

CHARLES DE GAULLE

France, 1890–1970

CHARLES DE GAULLE HAS COME to symbolize France more than any other individual of the 20th century. The commander of the Free French forces in the Second World War and the man most responsible for rebuilding his nation during the postwar years, de Gaulle himself best described his immense contribution to his homeland with the words "Je *suis* la France"—"I *am* France."

Charles-André-Marie-Joseph de Gaulle was born in Lille, France, on November 23, 1890. His father, a veteran of the Franco-Prussian War, imbued Charles with the patriotism and national pride that guided him throughout his life. The younger de Gaulle naturally turned to a military career as the best way to serve his homeland and entered the national military academy at Saint-Cyr in 1909.

Upon his graduation in 1912 Charles was commissioned a lieutenant in the infantry and assigned to staff duties under Gen. Henri Pétain. During the First World War, he served with distinction as an infantry captain, winning several citations for valor. Seriously wounded at the Battle of Verdun in 1916, Captain de Gaulle was captured and held as a prisoner of war in Germany for the duration of the Great War.

After the war de Gaulle resumed his military career as an officer in the Tank Corps, eventually rising to the rank of brigadier general. During these years he campaigned unsuccessfully for increased mobile strike forces for the army, alienating the French high command with his concerns about the value of the heavily fortified but static Maginot Line, concerns which proved justified when the Nazi tanks streamed around its northern flank into France in 1940.

(Above) Charles de Gaulle, the aristocratic and fiercely independent president of France in 1967.

(Opposite top) De Gaulle in full combat gear in front of his tank during the Nazi invasion of France in 1940. At the beginning of the war he was the French Army's top armored artillery strategist.

(Opposite) De Gaulle receives the salute of the citizens of Laval, France, following the town's liberation.

Charles de Gaulle quickly rose to national prominence during the Nazi onslaught when his Fourth Armored Division stood virtually alone against the German advance toward Calais. Promoted to general and named undersecretary of defense, he steadfastly refused to accept Marshal Pétain's surrender on June 21 or his collaborationist government at Vichy, escaping instead to England where he organized a Free French campaign against the Nazis. In the years that followed, de Gaulle's unbending resolve and personal magnetism held together the heroic Resistance movement in occupied France and the anti-Vichy underground in her North African colonies, paving the way for the Allied victories in these vital regions.

On August 20, 1944, in the wake of the D-Day invasion of Europe in June 1944 de Gaulle triumphantly returned to France and assumed the reins of government as premier. The compromise of politics did not appeal to the autocratic general, however, and he resigned in January 1946. Called out of retirement by popular demand in 1958, he served briefly as premier and then as president with enhanced powers, pursuing a "France first" policy that led to his nation's withdrawal from NATO in 1966. Upon the loss of a national referendum in April 1969 de Gaulle resigned and retired to his home at Colombey-les-Deux-Eglises, where he died on November 10, 1970. His successor as president, Georges Pompidou, best described the loss when he said, "De Gaulle is dead. France is a widow."

Field Marshal Bernard Montgomery, wearing his trademark black beret.

FIELD MARSHAL Bernard Montgomery was the United Kingdom's finest army commander during World War II. Brash and colorful, Monty was an inspiration to the war-torn English people and has entered modern military legend as the quintessential British officer.

Bernard Law Montgomery was born in London on November 17, 1887, the son of Anglican clergyman Henry Montgomery. He was raised, however, in Hobart, Tasmania, where his father was appointed bishop in 1889. After his return to London in 1901 the future field marshal attended St. Paul's School and the Royal Military Academy at Sandhurst and was commissioned a lieutenant in the Royal Warwickshire Regiment in 1908. Montgomery developed his reputation as a tough field commander early in the First World War, when he was badly wounded leading an attack at the First Battle of Ypres in 1914. He earned the coveted Distinguished Service Order for his actions in this engagement. By war's end he was

(Opposite) Monty on the shores of Normandy, June 1944. His British and Canadian troops secured three beachheads near Caen while the Americans were landing farther to the west.

Montgomery aboard an amphibious DUKW during his 8th Army's invasion of eastern Sicily in July 1943. His success in this campaign led to his appointment as British commander for Operation Overlord five months later.

(Opposite) Montgomery (right) accepts the surrender of the Nazi forces in northern Germany, the Netherlands, and Denmark at his headquarters at Luneburg Heath, Germany, on May 4, 1945.

a lieutenant colonel, and by 1937 he had risen to the rank of brigadier general.

At the beginning of the Second World War Montgomery was promoted to major general and given command of the Third Army Division in France. During the retreat to Dunkirk in May 1940, he kept his unit together in the face of overwhelming German attacks and tremendous confusion, marking him as one of Britain's top combat leaders. As a result in July 1942 he was named lieutenant general in charge of the British forces in Egypt, forces that had been badly defeated by Erwin Rommel's Afrikakorps.

Montgomery immediately began rebuilding his shattered command, and within weeks the flamboyant general had reoutfitted his troops and improved their morale. Although Monty had had no formal training in armored tactics he proved a natural at mechanized warfare and led his men to victory against a Nazi assault at Alam Halfa in September 1942. Taking the offensive in November he decisively defeated Rommel at El Alamein in northwest Egypt. In the months that followed, Montgomery— by then knighted and promoted to field marshal—pushed Rommel's forces back through Libya and then northward into Tunisia, scoring crushing victories at Medenine and then at Mareth in March 1943. The Afrikacorps was bagged in May between Gen. Dwight D. Eisenhower's forces and those of Montgomery. It was a big catch, but Rommel himself managed to elude capture.

Field Marshal Montgomery next led his Eighth Army across the Mediterranean, invading Sicily with U.S. Gen. George S. Patton's forces on July 10 and moving onto the Italian mainland on September 3. In December, however, Monty was reassigned to lead the Allied ground forces in the forthcoming invasion of Normandy. Working under Supreme Allied Commander Eisenhower, Monty prepared much of the battle plan for D-Day. During that campaign his armor skillfully kept Rommel's Panzer divisions away from the American bridgehead. Later Monty's force spearheaded the Allied drive into northern Belgium in September 1944. Following the Battle of the Bulge that winter, in which he played a key role, Monty crossed the Rhine and drove into the Ruhr, finally forcing the surrender of the northern German armies on May 4, 1945.

The field marshal was elevated to Viscount Montgomery of Alamein on January 31, 1946. He spent the years that followed as deputy commander of NATO and chief of the British General Staff, retiring from the army in September 1958 after 50 years of service. Field Marshal Lord Montgomery died at his home in Islington, England, on March 24, 1976.

MARSHAL

PHILIPPE PÉTAIN

France, 1856–1951

PHILLIPE PÉTAIN IS THE most controversial figure of modern French military history. One of the greatest heroes of the First World War, he and his accomplishments have been totally overshadowed by his collaboration with the Nazis as head of Vichy France during World War II.

Pétain was born in Cauchy-à-la-Tour, France, on April 24, 1856. A graduate of the French military academy at Saint-Cyr, he was commissioned an officer in the Chasseurs Alpins in 1878. Within a few years he developed a reputation as a good defensive strategist and was appointed an instructor at the Ecole de Guerre in 1888, serving there and in various staff positions for the next 25 years.

At the outbreak of the First World War, Pétain had no experience as a field commander. Nevertheless, France's pressing need for officers led to his promotion to brigadier general of infantry on August 31, 1914. He quickly proved that he was no mere armchair theorist, distinguishing himself at the First Battle of the Marne that September and then rapidly rising to division and corps command. By June 1915 he was named a full general and placed in charge of France's Second Army.

Pétain's greatest victory occurred at the Battle of Verdun in 1916, when he was assigned to defend that fortress town against a major German offensive begun on February 21. Vowing "they shall not pass," General Pétain held Verdun for months until finally in December the German High Command called off the campaign. Although incredibly costly—the French alone suffered more than 377,000 casualties—Pétain's victory stood as a symbol of France's resolve and made him a national hero. When the Allied war effort in Europe stalled in 1917 bringing threats of mutiny from the French troops, Pétain was named the new commander in chief of the French forces. Addressing the men's grievances, he quickly improved morale, and within months his popularity among the troops was exceeded only by that of the supreme Allied commander, Marshal Ferdinand Foch.

At the close of the war Pétain was promoted to marshal and appointed to the

Conseil Superieur de Guerre. While serving in this capacity during the 1920s he was instrumental in the creation of the Maginot Line, the 125-mile string of fortifications along the German border that epitomized his theories of defensive warfare. Pétain resigned from the army in 1931 to enter politics, eventually serving as minister of war and ambassador to Spain.

Following the German invasion of France in 1940—an invasion which Pétain's highly touted Maginot Line failed to halt—the aged marshal was asked to negotiate an armistice with Hitler's government. On behalf of his country, Pétain accepted the partitioning of France, with the north occupied by German troops and the south administered by a collaborationist government in Vichy that he agreed to head. At the end of the war he was convicted of treason by the Free French government and sentenced to death, a punishment subsequently commuted to life in prison by his former Verdun subordinate, Gen. Charles de Gaulle. Philippe Pétain died while still confined on the Ile d'Yeu on July 23, 1951.

(Above) Marshal Philippe Pétain wearing France's highest military award, the Médaille Militaire.

(Below) Pétain (seated center) during his trial for treason in July–August 1945. Condemned to death, he was subsequently given life in prison by the Free French leader Charles deGaulle.

MARSHAL GEORGI ZHUKOV stands high on the list of outstanding field commanders of the Second World War. Tough and resolute, he successfully coordinated some of the war's longest and most difficult campaigns, including the Soviet defenses of Moscow and Stalingrad.

Georgi Konstantinovich Zhukov was born in Strelkovka, Russia, in December 1896. During the First World War he served as a noncommissioned officer in the Tsarist Novgorod Dragoons, becoming in 1918 a leading officer in Leon Trotsky's Red Army. Remaining in the Russian Infantry at the close of the Revolution, Zhukov's tremendous natural talent earned him appointment to the Soviet Military Academy and promotion to general. In 1939 he became a national hero by decisively defeating a Japanese thrust into Mongolia, that convinced them not to attack the USSR during the Second World War. Recognized as one of the Soviet Union's best commanders, Zhukov was subsequently appointed Joseph Stalin's chief of staff in January 1941.

After Hitler's devastating sneak attack on Russia that June General Zhukov coordinated the entire defensive effort for Stalin. Although he successfully halted the German advance on Leningrad, he was dismissed as chief of staff for advocating a Soviet retreat from Kiev. Following the Red Army's devastating losses there in September he was reappointed by Stalin and charged with the defense of Moscow. By the end of the year the general had succeeded in driving the Nazis from the gates of the Soviet capital, for which he was named Deputy Supreme Commander of the Red Army.

Zhukov continued distinguishing himself in the years to follow. He led the dogged defense of Stalingrad starting in September 1942 and planned the surprise counteroffensive in November that led to the encirclement of the Nazi's Sixth Army and its surrender on February 2, 1943. Promoted to marshal, Zhukov next directed the campaign in the Ukraine, where his victory at the huge Battle of Kursk in July marked the turning point of the war on Hitler's eastern front. Following this victory, Zhukov continued relentlessly pressing the Nazis westward until, on May 2, 1945, he captured Berlin, effectively ending the war in Europe.

After the war Marshal Zhukov's popularity caused the mistrustful Stalin to demote him to an insignificant post where he was out of the public eye. Zhukov briefly regained prominence following Stalin's death in 1953, serving as minister of defense, but was ousted for political reasons in 1957. Georgi Zhukov died in Moscow on June 18, 1974.

Soviet Marshal Georgi Zhukov, the inspired commander who led the Russian armies to victory on the Eastern Front in World War II.

LIEUTENANT GENERAL
MARK CLARK
United States, 1896–1984

GEN. MARK CLARK WAS one of the United States Army's finest field commanders during the Second World War. Although his role during the conflict was overshadowed by those of Eisenhower, Patton, and Bradley in France and Germany, Clark's hard-hitting, 20-month campaign to secure Italy stands as a major achievement in the Allied victory in Europe.

Mark Wayne Clark was born in Madison Barracks, New York, on May 1, 1896, the son and grandson of career army officers. He was raised at army bases where his father, Col. Charles Clark, was commander, and entered West Point as a cadet in 1913. Commissioned an infantry lieutenant upon his graduation in 1917, he was assigned to duty in France with the 11th Infantry and was wounded in the fighting at Vosges in June 1918.

After he returned to the United States in 1919 Clark settled into the routine of a peacetime officer, serving in posts throughout the country and attending the Army Command School and War College. Following Pearl Harbor he was appointed chief of staff of the army ground forces headquarters in Washington, D.C., and by June 1942 was a major general on Gen. Dwight D. Eisenhower's staff in England. Assigned to "Operation Torch," the invasion of North Africa planned for that fall, Clark made a daring submarine landing in Morocco in October to gather intelligence and seek support among the Vichy French officers there. His mission not only provided Eisenhower with invaluable information for his November landings but succeeded in convincing Adm. Jean Darlan, commander of the collaborationist Vichy forces in North Africa, to order the surrender of all French troops in Morocco and Algeria.

Clark's success in North Africa earned him promotion to lieutenant general, making him at age 46 the youngest general staff officer in the service. He was also placed in command of the U.S. Fifth Army, which was being organized for the invasion of Italy. Following the capture of Sicily by Generals Patton and Montgomery in August 1943 Clark led his troops onto the mainland at Salerno on September 9, inspiring his men with a fearless frontline command style that won him the Distinguished Service Cross. Proceeding up the west coast of Italy while the British Eighth

An oil portrait of Gen. Mark Clark, painted in 1946 by Pietro Annigoni.

(Opposite) Clark (in front seat) parades past St. Peter's Basilica in June 1944, after his 5th Army's liberation of Rome. Seated behind him are his chief of staff, Gen. Alfred Gruenther, and his 2nd Corps commander, Gen. Geoffrey Keyes.

Army secured the east coast, Clark advanced northward until he was stopped by stiff German resistance at Monte Cassino in January. Swinging around the Nazi position, he made an amphibious landing at Anzio on January 22. He was held there until spring but broke the German line on May 23, captured Rome on June 4, and continued his advance up the Italian peninsula toward Bologna. At the end of the year he was named commander of all Allied forces in Italy, directing the troops in their final push to the Alps, where he accepted the trapped Germans' surrender on May 2, 1945.

Promoted to full general, Clark was appointed head of the U.S. occupation forces in Austria, where he remained until 1949. In 1952 he succeeded Gen. Matthew Ridgway as commander in chief of the U.N. forces in Korea, and in that capacity signed the armistice that ended the Korean War on July 27, 1953. Three months later, he retired from active duty to become president of the Citadel, a military academy in Charleston, South Carolina. He died in Charleston on April 17, 1984.

INDEX

PHOTO CREDITS

The Bettmann Archive 32, 37 (top & bottom), 47, 58, 59, 64, 68, 69, 78, 85, 92, 92–93, 102, 112, 128–129, 135, 141, 157, 161, 164 (bottom); Anne S. K. Brown Military Collection, Brown University Library 18, 48, 56, 70, 79, 84, 88, 97, 106, 140, 147, 156, 159, 162, 163; FPG International 143; Photograph by Gittings 89; Imperial War Museum, London 30, 49; The Kobal Collection 62, 63; Library of Congress 13, 14, 25, 38, 40, 42, 86, 90, 94–95, 99, 109, 110, 111, 116, (top), 117, 120, 125, 133, 138, 139, 142, 146, 170 (top); National Archives 2–3, 4–5, 6, 9–10, 15, (top & bottom), 23, 24, 27, 28–29, 33, 36, 44, 50, 51 (top & bottom), 52–53, 57, 60–61, 65, 72, 73, 74, 76, 76–77, 80, 81, 91, 107, 131 (top & bottom), 137, 144, 155, 160, 164 (top), 170 (bottom), 171; National Portrait Gallery, Smithsonian Institution 12, 22, 55, 172; Naval Photographic Center 20; Reuters/Bettmann 100; Photographic Section, Royal Air Force Museum 83; Super-Stock 82; UPI/Bettmann Newsphotos 16, 17, 19, 20–21, 28, 34, 35, 41, 43, 46, 54, 66, 67, 71, 75, 86–87, 96, 98, 101, 103, 104, 105, 108, 113, 114, 115, 118 (top & bottom), 119, 121, 122, 123, 124, 126, 127, 130, 132, 134, 136, 145, 148, 149, 150–151, 152, 153, 154, 158, 165, 166, 167, 168, 169, 173; War Memorial Museum of Virginia 116 (bottom); West Point Museum Collections, United States Military Academy, West Point, New York 26, 31, 39, 45.